P9-EAI-474

Dizzy Gillespie and the Birth of Bebop

R

leslie gourse

DIZZY GILLESPIE

and the Birth of Bebop

ATHENEUM BOOKS FOR CHILDREN

Atheneum 1994 New York

Maxwell Macmillan Canada
Toronto
Maxwell Macmillan International
New York Oxford Singapore Sydney

and Gail Paris, for nurturing this book.

from *To BE or Not . . . to BOP* by Dizzy Gillespie, copyright © 1979 by John Birks Gillespie and Wilmot Alfred Fraser, used by permission of Doubleday, a division of Bantam Doubleday Dell Publishing Group, Inc.

Atheneum
Macmillan Publishing Company
866 Third Avenue
New York, NY 10022

Maxwell Macmillan Canada, Inc.
1200 Eglinton Avenue East
Suite 200
Don Mills, Ontario M3C 3N1

Macmillan Publishing Company is part of the Maxwell Communication Group of Companies.

First edition
Printed in the United States of America
10 9 8 7 6 5 4 3 2 1
The text of this book is set in 12 pt. Weiss.

Library of Congress Cataloging-in-Publication Data
Gourse, Leslie.
Dizzy Gillespie and the birth of bebop / by Leslie Gourse.—1st ed.
p. cm.
Includes bibliographical references.
ISBN 0-689-31869-3
1. Gillespie, Dizzy, 1917– —Juvenile literature. 2. Jazz musicians—United States—Biography—Juvenile literature. 3. Bop (Music)—History and criticism—Juvenile literature.
[1. Gillespie, Dizzy, 1917– 2. Musicians. 3. Afro-Americans—Biography. 4. Bop (Music)] I. Title.
ML3930.G47G6 1994
788.9′2165′092—dc20
[B] 93-30222

For Trumpeter John "Tasty" Parker

contents

1

"i'd like to be known as a major messenger"

IN 1940 racial segregation was strictly enforced in most of the United States. Even so, an African-American jazz band leader and singer named Cab Calloway, who made recordings and toured the country to play for dances, became so popular that he had countless fans of all races. He earned so much money that one of his band members would reminisce about how Cab stuffed the bass fiddle cases and the drum set heads to carry all the money when the band traveled.

Cab's schedule in 1940 took him to Kansas City, Missouri, for a one-night stand to play in a theater. For him, it was going to be just another profitable night. He would dance in his billowing white tails, shake his head and send his long black hair flying, and sing about Minnie the Moocher, a hootchy-kootch dancer, "hi de hi de hi de ho." That was his biggest hit. He had made it popular in the famous Cotton Club in New York City's Harlem. Then audiences everywhere loved it and loved to dance to Cab's music.

Kansas City was filled with nightclubs in 1940, because the most important politician there, a man named Boss ("Big Tom") Pendergast, made sure that everything was available for people looking for pleasure—gambling, drinking, and sexual thrills. A Kansas City blues singer wrote a song about how he was living dangerously, having a love affair with another man's wife, who owned a big brass bed. Customers enjoyed that type of song. Boss Pendergast accepted bribes to keep the vices safe and the customers happy. While he ran Kansas City, it was one of the most corrupt places in the country. Music certainly wasn't the reason that tourists from all over the Midwest went there. But people did like to hear music while they gambled, drank, wheeled and dealed, and romanced. The hot, exciting, rhythmic music called jazz, or swing, provided a background sound for the people who used Kansas City as a playground.

Most jazz musicians in Kansas City didn't earn much money. Furthermore, most of them were African American, and the city was segregated. Their living conditions were often an indignity. But they liked to play there because many of their most talented colleagues flocked to town to hear and play the latest songs in clubs open twenty-four hours a day. The most famous jazz musicians—Cab Calloway for one—played one-night stands in Kansas City theaters for big fees.

Cab had an energetic, twenty-three-year-old trumpeter named Dizzy Gillespie in the band. Dizzy could play very high notes and had a driving style. For him, the Kansas City job with Cab would turn out to be a historic occasion in his life and for the development of jazz.

Dizzy was madly in love with music. As a boy in school, he had played his instrument even when his band teacher had been talking, trying to tell him what to do. By the time he was working in Cab's band, Dizzy had become such a good musician that he was experimenting with new musical accents and techniques. He loved to improvise—to choose unusual notes and invent complicated musical phrases to embellish old, familiar songs. His boldness led him to execute great leaps between high and low notes, and he could play trumpet faster than nearly anybody else in jazz. He skittered up and down the scales with lightning speed, screaming and burning on the horn. Dizzy played so swiftly that his notes had overtones that sounded like more notes than he was actually playing. He explored the possibilities of his trumpet continually, testing to see what he could play that nobody had ever played before.

His cousin, Norman Powe, who played trombone and had grown up with Dizzy in Cheraw, South Carolina, would one day say he had noticed how unusual Dizzy's playing was even when Dizzy was a teenager. He was always full of bright ideas. "I knew Dizzy was a genius, playing things that didn't sound right to me. I was just this blues man. He was doing things you wouldn't ordinarily hear," Norman said.

The fancy, intensely emotional style that Dizzy was developing for himself annoyed Cab Calloway. Many other great swing era bandleaders and musicians agreed with Cab. The bands in those days played predictable, syncopated, four-beat rhythms intended for dancing and derived from Dixieland—New Orleans music. That music, at the roots of jazz, had a simple, two-beat rhythm. Sometimes the unusual notes and new harmonies played by Dizzy sounded to Calloway as if Dizzy were playing wrong notes. Musicians loved to gossip to each other, and they passed along Cab's opinion. It became a legend in the jazz world. And so did Dizzy's brash style.

Dizzy loved to sit down at a piano and experiment with changing the notes in the chords of the old, standard songs. "I was always a chord freak," he would later say. "My style developed from the piano." On the trumpet, he could play only one note at a time. He used the new notes he found easily on the piano to insert in the melody lines he played on his trumpet. That way, he created a new mood and greater excitement when he went onstage.

Eventually, the substitute notes would lead him and other young, modern musicians to go so far as to invent whole new chords and melody lines. The new melody lines sometimes grew to be entirely new songs. The style of playing would have its own name by 1944: bebop. Milt Shaw, who became Dizzy's manager in 1947, in the period when Dizzy finally became popular, explained to a writer for *Esquire* magazine how the artistic music got its odd name. "When

Diz started playing bebop with a group, all their stuff was head arrangements—memorized material that wasn't written down. The pieces didn't have names. So Diz would [call out and imitate] the first phrases something like this: bee—bobba—do—bobba—doddle—dee—bebop! You know how many bebop choruses end in a clipped two-note phrase with the last note on an offbeat? It almost sounds like the instrument is saying bebop."

In Kansas City in 1940 Dizzy was about to meet a musician with whom he had a great deal in common. That musician was Charlie Parker, a twenty-year-old alto saxophonist nicknamed "Yardbird." "Bird," as he was usually called, also embellished songs to an astounding degree. Bird played more notes at faster speeds than anyone else, except for Dizzy. Bird, too, chose notes that produced unusual harmonies. He took his clues about which new notes to play from the original chords of old popular songs. Of great importance for his style, he played with more fluidity than anyone else could manage at his breakneck speed. Dizzy would one day say that Bird played notes other people couldn't even hear. Bird's phrasing and bluesiness would make a strong, lingering impression on Dizzy. He would later reflect that those aspects of Bird's playing were the reasons his style—and bebop itself—became so beloved by other musicians and jazz fans. "Charlie Parker came on the scene with the definition of phrasing. And then that was it," Dizzy remembered.

Dizzy and Bird became leaders in the new jazz style, bebop. They and their followers spent several years in the 1940s developing it. Most older musicians talked about how they disliked the new music. Audiences, too, were sometimes puzzled. And critics usually hated it. A young bebop musician might end a song on a low, sad-sounding, minor note, while an older, swing era musician finished on a high, happy, major note. Bebop musicians used sad-sounding flatted fifths all the time. (The fifth note of the scale in any key, when played as a flat, is a flatted fifth.)

The new harmonies that Dizzy, Bird, and their followers brought into jazz in the 1940s had already been introduced into classical European music some years earlier. Dizzy, for one, was well aware of the harmonies in European music. In audiences for classical music, too, not everybody liked the new, dissonant sounds and the plaintive feelings expressed by modernists. But the world was changing. Music could not remain untouched and distant from public events. The most progressive musicians in classical, jazz, and pop paid attention to world conditions and tried to express their feelings about life through music.

The United States was just emerging from a terrible financial depression. People had lost fortunes and savings, dreams and illusions in the 1929 stock market crash. Then the brutal World War II started. Asian, African, and European nations and the United States and Canada were in turmoil. People were confused and worried when Dizzy and a few other young musicians started experimenting with music and making it more elaborate and sophisticated. The new, more intense style of jazz reflected the struggle engulfing the world.

There was a special ingredient in Dizzy's and all the beboppers' music. Alone among the arts, jazz was primarily the invention of African Americans. It was syncopated, improvised music combining African rhythms, European harmonies, and American Indian and Caribbean influences. In the early part of the twentieth century, African-Americans had brought their genius for improvising out of the black churches in the United States. They had changed the words of the gospel songs and had sung the blues to express their feelings about all of life's experiences. Jazz, which evolved from the blues, gained in force and complexity, and reflected, among other things, the spirit of protest by African Americans against segregation and all social conditions related to racial prejudice.

So Dizzy's and Bird's new jazz style, bebop, would not simply be more complex, more artistic and sophisticated than its folk and swing era musical roots. Bebop would also express the anger and impatience of African Americans against racial prejudice. The new style of music would soon touch the life of every jazz musician of every race and religion in the world, and would inspire the musicians to keep adding breadth, depth, and variety to jazz. The struggles of jazz musicians were extremely difficult, but their musical blend, based primarily on African rhythms and European harmonies, helped bring about a greater measure of racial tolerance and equality. This music expressed the yearning of people everyplace to be free and independent, to reach out and communicate with one another, and to understand and enjoy one another's common humanity.

Jazz was the ideal vehicle for African-American musicians and their supporters to use to cry out for social changes. Jazz was entertainment. Everyone loved the swing era's syncopated, African-inspired rhythms, which continued in more complicated, insistent form in bebop.

Dizzy, a relaxed-looking man with an easy smile, didn't have any idea how important his meeting with Bird was. Eventually it would be Dizzy, above all, who taught other musicians how to play bebop, or progressive jazz, who wrote and arranged compositions, and who listened to Bird's compositions and wrote down the notes for Bird. Dizzy's methods and lifestyle were very different from Bird's. Parker was a slave to his bad habits; he drank too much alcohol, and he used heroin. When he tried to stop using heroin, he drank even more than usual, and he used Benzedrine, too. His addictions gave him ulcers and other serious medical problems.

Dizzy overcame every physical, mental, spiritual, and financial obstacle that he found in his way and devoted his life to developing and popularizing the new music. He never let any vice interfere with his music. He loved Bird, however, because of Bird's genius and his personal gentleness. Dizzy would always refer to Bird as "the other half of my heartbeat." When it came to music, that was true. The world would never be able to separate completely Dizzy's musical contribution from Bird's, so powerful was their collaboration.

Bird told his musician friends, who begged him to straighten out his life, that he had been put on earth primarily to demonstrate the evils of drug addiction. He died in 1955 at the age of thirty-four, a victim of drugs. Dizzy lived to be seventy-five years old. He saw bebop become world famous. And he inspired all jazz musicians to try to use every ounce of their spirits to keep elevating and asserting jazz as a major influence on and partner to all the arts. A tireless, affectionate teacher, Dizzy institutionalized the credo of all jazz musicians: Search for a new way.

In the 1950s and 1960s musicians who learned from Dizzy would improvise music from scales not normal in Western music. Some musicians played louder and bluesier music and turned to electronic instruments, while others emphasized European values for their bebop-based, swinging music. California jazz musicians played a relaxed, muted style of bebop known as "cool jazz." Still other musicians, inspired by the idea of trying something new, decided to play anything they pleased, without respect to the chords or scales. They called their sometimes atonal, wild music "free jazz."

Dizzy listened to all the music that evolved from bebop. He proudly concluded: "The message is descended from me. . . . I'd like to be known as a major messenger to jazz. . . . And since . . . [our] music . . . has come this far, it must have been something pretty important. The role of music goes hand in hand with social reformation—the changing of society to make things right, because music is a form of worship . . . music and musicians must help to set things right."

2

starting small

THE first photos of Dizzy Gillespie, born at home on October 21, 1917, show that he was a beautiful baby. When he grew to be a man, he looked at them with pride. But as a child, he didn't have the luxury of concentrating on how cute he was. He was the last of nine children born to a poor family in rural Cheraw, South Carolina. First he had to survive the threat of all the possible illnesses that could take the lives of babies in those days before modern medicine. In Cheraw, there was only one county hospital serving several thousand people. As a "colored" child (that was the polite conversational way of referring to African Americans in those days), Dizzy would not have been able to get medical attention at that segregated hospital. He had to rely upon the resources of his family and the African-American community for medical care. And he had to learn to thrive in a family where his father, James Gillespie, was a strict disciplinarian. Many people thought Dizzy's father was just plain mean.

Every Sunday morning, Dizzy woke up to hear his father yelling for him and his elder brother Wesley to get their weekly beatings. Their father hit them with a leather strap. Dizzy, who was then called by his baptismal name, John Birks Gillespie, and Wesley, the Gillespie child closest in age to Dizzy, suffered through the beatings courageously—or at least with spirit. Dizzy sometimes tried to hide under the bed, shouting, "But I didn't do anything!" His father insisted the beatings were for all the things that he must have done wrong during the week. One of Dizzy's eldest brothers, James Penfield Gillespie, called "J. P.," was so upset by his father's strictness that he ran away from home. Dizzy was about five years old at the time. Soon after J. P. left, Sonny, another brother, moved to Philadelphia, where he died in his mid-thirties. Dizzy was still a teenager then in Cheraw, and never got a chance to know Sonny well.

From about 1922 Dizzy grew up in a house with Wesley and their three sisters. As the last-born Gillespie child, he may have been his mother's pet. But Dizzy thought his sister Eugenia couldn't stand him. She used to pinch and harass him, and one day she pushed him out a window. Dizzy fell on his head and bled a lot. He ran to his mother and told her that Eugenia had pushed him, but his mother didn't believe him. Although Eugenia was popular as a baby-sitter, and many of Dizzy's mother's friends left their kids with her, it seems she had little patience or goodwill then toward Dizzy, who was a mischievous daredevil.

Eugenia could remember a time when he climbed up on a cabinet full of dishes and jars and knocked it over on himself. She, her mother, and the rest of the family pulled him free of the wreckage, worrying that he was dead. But they found him laughing—with jam all over his face! The kids had all worked hard to pick berries, and their mother had worked hard to make that jam.

He would later attribute his "hotheadedness," as he called it, to his father's meanness. Those beatings and Eugenia's bullying taught Dizzy early in life to fight for himself, to be tough and not to expect the world to coddle and protect him. As an African American, he could be subject to abuse from gangs of whites who might try to beat him up just because he was walking down the street. Dizzy fought to defend himself against African Americans, too. He didn't want people to get the idea they could take advantage of him. The beatings by his father trained him to be alert and to survive unreasonable, unexpected disasters.

Dizzy admired and respected his tough, stubborn father. And Dizzy tried to imitate and please the elder Gillespie because his father was a staunch family man, a hard worker, and a devoted amateur musician.

James Gillespie worked as a bricklayer five days a week in the old Anderson brickyard. Sometimes he came home on payday with his white work overalls stuffed with candies. His kids crawled all over him, picking the candies out of his pockets, while he laughed with delight. He was also very generous with his wife, and he brought her presents whenever he could. Dizzy had no memory of his father ever hitting his mother, Lotte Powe Gillespie.

Dizzy also had happy memories of some of his numerous relatives. His mother's father, whom Dizzy called Paw, used to take a few drinks with a friend at the end of every week. They stood outside Paw's house, singing comic songs aloud, although it was illegal for African Americans to sing loudly in public. Paw didn't really make too much noise, but he liked to give the illusion that he was breaking the law. Paw's example taught Dizzy to have a sense of humor. Dizzy grew up loving to laugh and tease people, just as his favorite men in the family did.

On weekends Dizzy's father played piano and led his own little band to earn more money. James Gillespie bought all the instruments himself and kept them in his house during the week, because the musicians in his band were so poor they might sell them. Cheraw didn't have a pawnshop. But some people found ways to pawn instruments with other people, and then those people would pawn them again. The original owner of an instrument had to go all over town looking for it when he needed it. With all the instruments in his own house—a piano, a guitar, a drum set, a mandolin, and a one-string bass fiddle—Dizzy had a chance to touch and feel them. He heard what they sounded like. His father made Dizzy's brothers and sisters learn to play and to practice, even though none of them had much interest in music.

Dizzy, however, was fascinated. He went to the house

of a neighbor, a schoolteacher, who tolerated his playing one song called "Coon Shine Lady" with two fingers, over and over again, on her piano. Finally she got tired of that and taught him the alphabet; he learned to count and to read, too. By the time he went to school when he was five, Dizzy knew all the lessons so well that he was bored in class. He started to whistle. The irritated teacher took a switch to his legs, and Dizzy ran all the way home. His father was so furious that he went to the principal's house and yelled that the teacher better not hit his kid again. Dizzy hid around the corner of the house and listened, thrilled and proud of how protective his father was. Soon Dizzy was promoted to a higher grade. Then he skipped another grade, so that he was in the same grade as his elder brother Wesley.

Their mother stayed busy raising seven remaining children, keeping the house in order, and putting meals on the table, while their father laid down the law. It would seem to later generations, steeped in lessons about the joys of gentle child-rearing, that Dizzy's father could be an unreasonable tyrant. In those days, parents who were strict disciplinarians and didn't hesitate to hit their kids were commonplace and normal. Dizzy was able to love his father despite those faults.

One sunny morning in June 1927, Dizzy watched Wesley leave the house early to pick blackberries. Soon afterward, a rabid dog, glassy eyed and frothing at the mouth, appeared in the Gillespies' yard. Dizzy's father sent Dizzy and the rest of the kids to a neighbor to fetch a gun. The neighbor came running and killed the dog, and the

Gillespies buried it. Then James Gillespie began to gasp for breath. He was having such a bad asthma attack that his wife put him to bed. Just then Wesley reappeared at the house. Some instinct had drawn him back early from berry picking. Suddenly they heard their mother crying in the bedroom. Their father had died.

After the funeral there was nothing else for Dizzy to do but go back to school. A classmate told him that his father had died and gone to hell. Dizzy immediately started a fight, one of many he would have during his lifetime.

The death of James Gillespie brought sudden poverty to the family. Cheraw was not a rich community. A small, rural place in northeastern South Carolina, it had sandy soil in a gently rolling countryside. Farmers had to work hard to grow their crops. James Gillespie had labored for a weekly wage. Mrs. Gillespie had always been a housewife. After he died, the Gillespies had no income. Their only breadwinner was gone.

Then the family's savings disappeared, too. Dizzy said they were stolen by a bank president in Cheraw in 1929. In the depression that hit the whole country, banks failed everyplace. Lotte Gillespie and her children were able to keep living in their clapboard house with a handful of rooms and a front porch in a neighborhood then strictly for African Americans. But with Cheraw's economy depressed, and all the facilities segregated, the Gillespies did not have opportunities to find good jobs.

Dizzy's mother started to do laundry for other families, and she never earned much money—about $1.50 a week. It wasn't enough to feed herself and the kids. They were often hungry. They were so ashamed of their ragged clothes that they hid out in the woods on Easter, pretending to have a picnic, so they didn't have to show up barefoot in their church.

They tried to help their mother. Wesley chopped so much wood for her to have kindling for fuel while she was ironing that he had nightmares about the work. Dizzy tried to comfort Wesley during the dark, frightening nights when their stomachs felt hollow and empty.

Dizzy became feisty and angry. Once he teased a boy, who retaliated by throwing an ax, which barely missed Dizzy. He and Wesley stole watermelons from a farmer, who fired at them with a shotgun. Dizzy misbehaved in school, too. Once he made a teacher so angry that she started to choke him. He threatened to hit her with an old-fashioned, heavy eraser, so she let go. When she realized the trouble he was having, she and her husband started feeding him meals, saving his life when he was ten years old.

Wesley Gillespie noticed that Dizzy was always eager to fight—and always ready to goldbrick when it came time to work. The brothers were supposed to pick cotton as one of their jobs to help earn money for the family. Wesley picked over a hundred pounds of cotton, while Dizzy picked only fifteen. When Wesley was working, Dizzy ate all the lunch their mother had prepared for them. Wesley complained to her. But Dizzy explained that he wasn't put on this earth to pick cotton, and he promised her: "Someday I'm gonna be a musician; you're going to be proud of me." For a long time, though, his mother could see no sign of Dizzy's coming greatness. Dizzy would later reflect he was a little surprised that he didn't get killed in those days, because he fought so fearlessly, frequently, and sometimes so foolishly.

The school system, too, helped save Dizzy's life. In the fifth grade, Dizzy volunteered to play in the school band run by Alice Wilson, the fourth-grade teacher. He was the youngest, smallest child to volunteer, and he was also one of the last to arrive in the instrument room. All that was left for him was a slide trombone. Nobody else wanted it. Far from being disappointed, Dizzy grabbed it. His arms were too short to move the slide out far enough to reach the positions to play the high notes. But he didn't mind. He practiced hard and alerted the whole neighborhood to his new love—playing music.

One day, as he was practicing at home, he heard the sound of a trumpet. His next-door neighbor, James "Son" Harrington, had been given a long, nickel-plated trumpet for a Christmas gift. Son's mother was the woman who had let Dizzy play her piano and had taught him the alphabet and other early lessons. Dizzy had never seen a trumpet before. His father had never had a trumpet in the house, in part because it wasn't a typical instrument to have in a southern, country-style band.

"Boy, I sure like the way that thing sounds," Dizzy told Son. Son was very generous with the trumpet and taught Dizzy to play the B-flat scale. From then on, Dizzy stayed close to Son, playing the trumpet whenever it wasn't in use. Mrs. Wilson began to notice that Dizzy—"a fidgety, frisky little fellow" as she called him—was happy as long as he could hold his instrument in his hands. Somehow he managed to acquire a cornet (a kind of trumpet) of his own, and he played it in the school play that Mrs. Wilson produced. While she gave instructions to the group, Dizzy kept playing his cornet, practicing scales. She couldn't make him listen.

He went to school every day with his cornet, not his books, under his arm. "His brother Wesley would have the books. They were in the same class, but John was smarter than Wesley," Mrs. Wilson noted about Dizzy. "He was a mess, but he was a loving child. All the children loved him, and so did the teachers that had anything to do with him. In a sense he was comical. Of course, we didn't call it that way then; we'd say he was 'crazy'! believed in fun. He was always full of fun. Yet he had his own individual style with everything. He was just like that, the way he held his horn. He'd try to hold it with one hand. Anything to show off. He's a show-off. That's the best way I can say it—a real show-off, but he was a good one."

As it happened, B-flat was the only key that Mrs. Wilson could play in. She taught all her students, including Dizzy, to use that key in a little group she organized for her yearly minstrel show. The audience applauded so much that the boys in her group decided to look for jobs that paid them. When they played for a dance at a white high school, Son Harrington let Dizzy borrow his trumpet. The boys bought stock arrangements for popular tunes of the day and made a big hit. They went on to get jobs playing for house parties, for dances at the Elks hall, and even for parties and dances in other little towns in the area and across the state border in Hamlet, North Carolina.

Dizzy fell so in love with music that he hung around anyplace in Cheraw where he could hear it. Even though Cheraw was segregated, Dizzy didn't worry about what color the people were at the places where he went. Whites got used to seeing him. He was invited inside to dance as an entertainer at "whites only" parties. Dizzy could do a dance he called "snake hips." When he undulated his way onto the dance floor, swaying his hips, people threw quarters at him. "Sometimes I'd make two or three dollars for just a few minutes. That was a lot of money for a young boy during the Depression to scoop up off a dance floor," he would recall. He also learned about music from watching white college boys play their instruments for parties. They used arrangements that they wrote themselves. That intrigued Dizzy.

He acquired the reputation for playing the cornet and trumpet better than anyone else in the area, and so he became very impressed with himself. Then a local musician, who had left Cheraw to live in Philadelphia, came back to visit his family. Dizzy heard about him and got set to have a contest to see who could play a certain popular song best. The visitor did a beautiful job, but Dizzy discovered he couldn't play the song at all, because all he knew was the key of B-flat. The song was written in a different key. Dizzy couldn't find one right note on the trumpet! The lesson was painful. Luckily, his cousin Norman Powe knew how to read music. Norman showed Dizzy some written trombone lessons, and he learned to play in keys other than B-flat.

One of the most important early musical influences on Dizzy was the Sanctified Church. Cheraw had many churches for all denominations, and because they were segregated, African Americans had many churches of their own. Dizzy, who was brought up as a Methodist, was not supposed to go to anybody else's church. The Sanctified Church was definitely off limits. It was considered an eccentric, low-class place of worship, because followers of the Sanctified religion "practiced spirit possession and speaking in tongues," Dizzy recalled.

Indiscreet though it was for Dizzy to go there, he sneaked in on Sunday nights to hear the music. He watched the people throw themselves body and soul into their religion, and he heard them make a joyful noise. The rhythmic music of the Sanctified Church services excited people and swept them away with religious fervor. With a cymbal, a bass drum, a snare drum, and a tambourine, musicians in the church kept four rhythms going at once. The congregation joined in, stomping their feet, clapping their hands, and jumping up and down on the wooden floor; they added more rhythms. Dizzy noticed that white people used to go, too, and sit outside in their cars just to listen to the hot music. "Everybody would be shouting and fainting and stomping. . . . The Sanctified church's rhythms got to me. . . . I received my first experience with rhythm and spiritual transport going down there. . . . I've followed it ever since," Dizzy later related. He would become famous for his use of rhythms, especially Afro-Cuban rhythms, in his conception of jazz.

With girls Dizzy had absolutely no talent. He tried to catch one pretty girl's attention by throwing rocks at her. She later married one of his cousins. Another girl that he liked was so bashful that she wouldn't even look at him. But he moved around town to all the places where he could hear or play music, and he continued to build his reputation as a trumpet star in Cheraw. He was always welcome at Son Harrington's house, and he liked to go because Mrs. Harrington owned a radio and a gramophone. The Gillespies couldn't afford either one. "That's how jive it felt to be poor," Dizzy later recalled.

He listened to a broadcast of Teddy Hill's jazz band from the Savoy Ballroom, a popular dance hall in Harlem in New York. Dizzy loved the sound of the band, and he especially adored Hill's exciting, intense trumpet player, Roy Eldridge. The first time Dizzy heard Roy Eldridge play his vibrant music with Hill, Dizzy said to himself, "Yeah, that's the man." Roy could play so many notes so fast that they sounded like vibrato, and he screamed on the high notes. Dizzy would remember all his life the way that the band played "Looky Looky Looky, Here Comes Cookie." Because he wanted to have the trumpet man's job in that band, Dizzy started patterning his playing after Eldridge's style. It would take a few more years, but Dizzy actually did get Eldridge's job.

At the time he was listening to that broadcast, Dizzy thought his situation was hopeless. He had no money to study music. He even had to drop out of school after he was graduated from the ninth grade, so that he could work on a road gang to earn money to help his family. He shoveled dirt and hated every minute of it. By then he was almost sixteen years old, upset and humiliated as he watched his illiterate "brothers," other African-American youngsters, sign for their pay by marking an X for their names. Dizzy forced himself to go to the job for the money. He kept his spirits up by playing trumpet and cornet around Cheraw.

3

a scholarship to high school

ABOUT twenty-eight miles away, the Laurinburg Technical Institute, an agricultural high school in North Carolina, had a school band. The trumpet and trombone players had just graduated, and so the school needed replacements. One of Dizzy's neighbors, who was studying nursing at Laurinburg, recommended Dizzy and his cousin Norman Powe, who played trombone.

Dizzy was shocked and thrilled to hear he was getting a scholarship to go to Laurinburg. Although it meant he would have to live away from his mother, he took only a minute to make up his mind. He was so poor that he walked and hitched rides from Cheraw to the school, carrying only a toothbrush, a towel, and a change of underwear. He didn't even own a trumpet. And, hungry as usual, he arrived at Laurinburg.

When Dizzy walked into his dormitory room, he found a teenage roommate from New York City who had plenty to wear. By the time they went to their first dinner in the school's mess hall, Dizzy was wearing some of his friendly, new roommate's clothes. In the mess hall, Dizzy noticed that one table of students had their plates heaped high with food, while all the other students had skimpy portions. Why was that? Dizzy wanted to know. Well, the best-fed students played for the football team, he found out.

Even though he was very small for his age, Dizzy boldly hurried to try out for the football team the next day. He put on the best uniform he could find in the locker room; but it quickly became clear to the coach that Dizzy had no skills or experience. The coach was ready to throw Dizzy off the team. But the little fellow's efforts to play impressed him. Every time he was yelled at, Dizzy imagined some extra pork chops on his plate, and he tried harder. So he was given an old uniform and allowed to join the team. One day he realized that if he had his teeth knocked out, or if he hurt his mouth in any way, he might not be able to play trumpet anymore. So Dizzy quit the football team instantly and went back to small portions of food.

Laurinburg was first and foremost an agricultural school. Dizzy did the farm-oriented schoolwork, but he detested it. He wasn't cut out to be a farmer, he knew. He liked the look of the healthy crops at the school and the livestock pens only because they made him think of the many meals he was living near.

He stayed in school because he was getting a little bit of musical education free of charge. It was a time for Dizzy to play music while he was being fed and housed. He didn't have to work on a road gang or do anything else but the schoolwork. The bandmaster had a hard time keeping the band going, because most of the players didn't read music. Dizzy could read; he also taught himself a little theory. "It was enough to get around musically," he later said. He played piano and trumpet day and night. His cousin Norman, who kept him company when he played, admired Dizzy's talent and endless appetite for music. Dizzy later reminisced: "I'd practice the trumpet and then the piano for twenty-four hours straight if they didn't come around and shut me up when they checked the locks every night."

He became so skilled from his constant work that some of the less-talented band members got on his nerves. He always hated it when anybody he played with let him down. Dizzy once corrected an error made by a huge tuba player, who decided to whip Dizzy instead of thank him. Dizzy, about a hundred pounds lighter than the tuba player, pulled out a knife. The big fellow backed away.

Soon afterward the school administrator called Dizzy to the office and asked if he had actually pulled a knife on the tuba player. Dizzy admitted it, explaining, "He could have hit me in my mouth and ruined my embouchure." (Embouchure is the method of applying the lips and tongue to the mouthpiece of a wind instrument. All horn players develop their muscles and techniques for their embouchure, so that they can play the horn. Horn players with mouth injuries have often found themselves unable to play anymore, or else they have had to learn new techniques, and often the new techniques are not as good as the old ones.) "I plan to go into music as a career, and I wouldn't be able to play." The administrator let Dizzy go. Dizzy thought he got off without punishment because he was so serious about music, and because he had obviously been acting in self-defense.

At Laurinburg the boys' and girls' dormitories were separate, but Dizzy managed to sneak into a girl's room one night at her invitation. His shyness with girls had ended. At parties he found he could impress them because he was so good at dancing; he was relaxed and amusing on the dance floor. On weekends he played for parties and dances that paid him. Sometimes he played with a school band, sometimes with area bands. Life became a whirl of music and fun, for whatever he played, he attracted the attention of the girls in the audiences. Sometimes he sneaked away with a girl for a few minutes of passionate kissing and romancing. And a few times he had to grab his clothes and run, chased away by jealous boyfriends.

He didn't fare very well in some of his courses in his senior year, and so he was asked to work on the school farm for the summer and repeat the courses the next semester. He earned a little money for his farmwork, but he was terribly bored. His mother, his sisters Mattie, Laura, and Eugenia, and his brother Wesley with his wife, Marjorie, had moved to Philadelphia that year, 1935. Dizzy was left alone in the South. He started thinking about dropping out of Laurinburg to join his family.

If it seemed to some people that Dizzy had a devil-may-care, irresponsible attitude toward life, his cousin Norman knew that Dizzy's mind was always on music. "Dizzy doesn't care about anything but the trumpet," Norman later said. Dizzy had settled on that very fast, intense trumpet style of Roy Eldridge, and sacrificed developing a pretty tone in favor of learning to execute the most difficult feats on that instrument. It could have been on his mind, as he was missing his family, that there were many opportunities to play music in a big, northern city such as Philadelphia. He might be able to get a job as a musician.

One day, visiting Cheraw, while staying with Norman's family, Dizzy saw a youngster drowning in a swimming pool. He jumped into the water and kept pushing the boy from underneath until the boy grabbed on to something and was able to get out of the water. In gratitude, the boy's brother, who had a car and was going north, offered to give Dizzy a ride to Philadelphia. Dizzy put all his belongings into a little knapsack. He had to leave the school trumpet behind, because it didn't belong to him. That was the end of his high school education.

4

that dizzy cat becomes a man

IN Philadelphia he discovered that everyone in his family had a job. The women did piecework in factories; Wesley, who would become a good chef, worked in a restaurant. Within three days of arriving in town, Dizzy auditioned for a job and got it. His sister Mattie's husband, Bill, took Dizzy to a pawnshop and bought him his first trumpet for thirteen dollars.

Dizzy played for eight dollars a week in a joint that was so rowdy it was later nicknamed "Pearl Harbor," Dizzy would recall. After about a month, he had bought himself three stylish suits and found another job—this one for twelve dollars a week. With his usual energetic, bright outlook, he easily made friends with the musicians he met in the Philadelphia clubs. That ability was a big boost for Dizzy. For musicians, the most important things happen through personal connections. Friends lead to jobs. Dizzy's professional struggle was under way in earnest. He practiced with musicians he met in the neighborhood. And the gregarious, family-loving Dizzy was also delighted to be living with his mother again.

Dizzy carried his trumpet around in a paper bag because his brother-in-law hadn't bought him a trumpet case. Dizzy didn't realize at first how funny his small-town, southern mannerisms and the paper bag looked to musicians in a big northern city. He was still introducing himself as John Birks Gillespie; no one had mentioned the nickname "Dizzy" yet.

In 1936 he was given the chance to try out for a popular Philadelphia band led by Frankie Fairfax. Dizzy didn't do well in the audition. He knew how to read printed stock orchestrations, which were clearly marked, but he couldn't decipher the badly notated arrangements written by hand in pencil for the Fairfax band. Most bands of the day used messy-looking arrangements written in pencil because the arrangers liked to keep the whole fee—usually seven dollars—for the arrangement and not have to share it with a copyist. Dizzy overheard Fairfax's pianist and arranger, Bill Doggett, refer to him as "that dizzy cat" when he couldn't read the pencil-written chart.

But the musicians knew that Dizzy could execute exciting things on his trumpet. So when Fairfax organized another band a little later, Dizzy was asked to join, with trumpeters Charlie Shavers and Carl "Bama" Warwick, two men who would also become important jazz players in the future. Charlie, Bama, and Dizzy became good friends and ran around to Philadelphia's music clubs together. They filled up on cheap meals in a soup kitchen run by Father Divine and taught one another about the trumpet.

Dizzy kept playing piano, too, because he knew how valuable it was for him to see all the notes as he was planning his trumpet work. Bill Doggett sometimes went to Dizzy's house and played trumpet while Dizzy played piano. Doggett noticed how Dizzy used the piano to help support and stretch his imagination when he searched for the best notes to play on the trumpet. Other trumpet players jammed with Dizzy in their free time, too. "I practiced all day every day, and pretty soon I was one of the boys in Philadelphia," he later recalled.

One night he was practicing the piano on a bandstand before a job with the Fairfax band. When the men were supposed to start playing, Dizzy had disappeared. One of the musicians—maybe Fairfax himself—yelled out, "Where's Dizzy, man?" Everybody laughed. Another musician in the band seconded the motion: "Yeah, that's a good name for that cat!" The name stuck.

When Dizzy stood up to play in the trumpet section, he sometimes danced. He always loved calling attention to himself. The other musicians laughed at him. They thought the reason he joked around so much was that he was just a kid. But nobody laughed at the way he played. He could play in any key, and he could already play faster and with more fire than most musicians ever did. On and off the bandstand, Dizzy knew, he was "excitable" and ready for anything.

When he found a bandmate asleep in a room filled with gas during a tour that the Fairfax band made in the South, Dizzy ran into the room and pulled the musician to safety. Dizzy was the same way on a bandstand. He didn't think twice about doing something if he thought it would breathe life into the music and the show. Nobody could predict what that dizzy cat was going to play to show himself off. He was becoming more adventurous as he became more sure of himself as a musician.

He went to hear famous musicians, such as Duke Ellington and Teddy Hill and their orchestras, and he got a chance to hear his idol, Hill's trumpeter, Roy Eldridge, in person at the Rendezvous Room. The club itself made a deep impression on Dizzy because it was very dark, the girls wore short, daring dresses, and Dizzy thought everybody there was out on a date with his neighbor's wife. He had never seen anything as flashy and seductive in the rural South.

Dizzy kept playing with the blues-based Fairfax dance band at the Strand Ballroom. A white woman who worked for a newspaper went to hear him play and followed him home every night. At first he refused to take the rides she offered him, because he was unaccustomed to being friends with a white woman. Down south, he wouldn't have dared to have a white girlfriend.

One night, after he agreed to get into her car, she immediately kissed him and started a little romance. Dizzy was relieved to discover that nobody bothered him about crossing the race line. In a big northern city, the social scene could be wide open. He didn't risk getting lynched because, for one thing, nobody paid close attention to him in the big city. Few people knew him. He also had an African-American girlfriend, with whom he felt more comfortable. Her mother owned a restaurant where Dizzy ate many hearty meals. He had no thought of getting married and settling down, however. Many nights he walked home alone from his job with the Fairfax band.

One night a car filled with young white men looking for a fight pulled up alongside Dizzy and tried to pick on him. He knew that gangs sometimes beat up African-American men, so he opened the knife he always kept in his pocket. When a white man reached out to grab him, Dizzy cut the man's hand badly. The man's friends had to call the fight off and speed their buddy to a hospital for stitches. As shocking as the story might seem, it was a part of Dizzy's everyday reality. He knew he had to be ready for anything.

One day he would reminisce: "In south Philly there were a lot of gangsters who used to grab little guys, little colored guys, off the street and beat 'em up and throw 'em out in the woods half dead. . . . It was still dangerous to mess with me then." (Many decades would pass before Dizzy's fighting days ended—before he felt secure enough to bypass a fight.)

Although he wasn't earning much money with the Fairfax band, Dizzy liked Philadelphia. So he stayed with Frankie Fairfax until 1937. During that time he heard the song "Good Night, My Love" sung by Ella Fitzgerald. Dizzy was inspired enough by the song to write an arrangement of it for the Fairfax band. He spent two and a half months on it—a long time. There was nobody to help him find his way. Writing parts for all the instruments, noting exactly where they came in, he produced an arrangement good enough to impress Fairfax. There were some good arrangers in the Fairfax band; Bill Doggett was one. So Dizzy was pleased to have his arrangement used at all.

Then he got a phone call from Bama and Charlie Shavers, who had moved on, asking him to come to New York and play for Lucky Millinder, the leader of a popular jazz band based there. Every young musician dreamed about going to New York and becoming a star. Dizzy felt tempted to leave home. His older brother J. P.—James Penfield Gillespie—had an apartment in the heart of Harlem, on West 142d Street between Seventh and Eighth avenues. Dizzy knew he could stay there. J. P. earned $12.50 a week, and Dizzy had saved some money while working in Philadelphia. J. P. had only one bed, however. When Dizzy came home at 4:00 A.M., J. P. got up and let Dizzy go to sleep. Then J. P. sat in the park until it was time for him to go to work. For a while, the arrangement suited J. P. very well. The brothers shared expenses.

Although Dizzy went on Lucky Millinder's payroll, he never actually played with the band at that time. Lucky had a trumpet player named Harry "Sweets" Edison who was supposed to be leaving. But Sweets was a wonderful player, with one of the prettiest tones and most fluid trumpet styles in all of jazz history. Sweets knew how to hesitate and then improvise a little sweet something for a tune.

Lucky decided to keep the distinctive player who would later play with Count Basie's famous band and become a legend in jazz. Lucky simply stopped paying Dizzy.

But New York excited Dizzy, and his brother was so hospitable that Dizzy didn't think once about going home to his mother. Charlie Shavers introduced Dizzy to many young players in Harlem, among them a drummer, Kenny Clarke, with whom Dizzy would have a very important musical relationship. With his new friends, he went to listen and jam (play for no pay) every night in clubs from Greenwich Village in lower Manhattan to Harlem up north.

Among Harlem's many popular clubs were Clark Monroe's Uptown House and Dickie Wells's Clam House, both after-hours places. They featured informally organized music groups after 4:00 A.M., when every bar was supposed to stop serving liquor. Visiting every place in Harlem, including the Savoy Ballroom, Dizzy began playing for more people with more varied interests and backgrounds than he had ever entertained before.

Dizzy met bandleader Teddy Hill at the Savoy, just at a time when Teddy was preparing to take a band to Europe and needed a trumpeter. Dizzy thought Teddy hired him because he sounded like Roy Eldridge, who had just left the Hill band. Although Dizzy would only be third trumpeter, he would get to see Europe. And the pay was seventy dollars a week—more than most people earned in those days. Dizzy, of course, jumped at the chance.

He was so inexperienced that he didn't know enough to point his trumpet at a microphone during a recording session with Hill's band in May 1937. All the musicians had to step forward to use the one microphone provided for their solos. Dizzy kept swinging from side to side, without giving the microphone a second thought, until Hill pointed to it. Dizzy liked that recording session because it was his first. Though he had been nervous, his efforts to be equal to a challenge, learn on the job, and perhaps play something memorable gave him a satisfied feeling then—and always. Of the six tunes recorded that day, "King Porter Stomp," with Dizzy's vivid, lively solo, became the best known. His brilliance showed up, too, on another song, "Blue Rhythm Fantasy," and more than made up for his behind-the-scenes awkwardness. Though he still imitated Roy Eldridge, Dizzy had a crisper, more abrupt approach, with more drive.

Teddy Hill not only liked Dizzy's modern approach to the trumpet, he liked Dizzy for personal reasons. Hill had a little daughter. Especially charming with children, Dizzy enjoyed playing with Hill's daughter and making her laugh. So Hill was willing to take a chance on the young trumpeter for a European tour.

Some of the men in the band, who had been playing together for years, threatened to quit if Teddy took Dizzy along, but Hill refused to give in to the pressure. The older musicians decided not to quit; but then they barely talked to Dizzy. It was typical of them to give newcomers a hard time.

Dizzy loved crossing the Atlantic on a ship, the *Île de France*. He was also enchanted by the six weeks he spent in Paris, performing at a famous club, the Moulin Rouge. He was upset, though, when he learned that the old guard in the band—jealous, cliquey, and competitive—refused to introduce him to record producers. The musicians told the French producers that the new trumpet player wasn't talented. Since he got no recording jobs, for which he would have been paid, Dizzy had to make the trip fun and worthwhile for himself in other ways.

There was one older musician whom Dizzy revered: Bill Dillard. The Hill band's first trumpeter, he was "one of the earliest guys to assist me. He'd show me . . . how to sing on the trumpet," Dizzy later recalled. He would always tell interviewers that Dillard had a sweet personality and helped everybody. Dillard taught Dizzy technical tricks that Dizzy used all his professional life: how to hold a note and how to decide to use a trilling vibrato or let a note come out to its full value. "The way that he taught was a joy," Dizzy later wrote. "I was young and fly and could play. I could read like hell, but I didn't know a lot of the fine points of music. Bill helped me change the little things that I did that weren't professional."

In charge of the brass section, Dillard noticed some unusual things about Dizzy's playing even then. Dizzy positioned his jaws in a strange way, so that his cheeks filled up with air like little balloons when he played. That was a poor technique, and Dizzy's cheek muscles finally lost their resilience. Each cheek blew up nearly as big as the rest of his head. This phenomenon would later be studied by medical science with the name "Gillespie's pouches." Dillard didn't try to make Dizzy change his embouchure. "The results were the only thing that mattered," Dillard later said.

Dillard especially admired Dizzy's ease and speed on the highest notes. And like Teddy Hill, Dillard loved Dizzy's cheerful personality. "He was always ready to laugh and giggle at the slightest thing," Dillard would recall.

> And his playing reflected that, too. Because I remember when I first heard him play, he would attempt to play something in the "stratosphere," and occasionally it didn't work out. He would take his horn down and laugh. . . . I realized that he was working out his thing, and he had the reckless kind of abandon to develop that type of style, where most of us had always been taught that you should be very careful and precise, make sure you didn't make any bad notes. If it's something that you thought might be a little too fast, play it slower, but play it clean and precise, you know. But you could never achieve what he was achieving with that conception. I think you have to have a reckless kind of abandon, at least when you're trying to develop in the early stages, or you would never accomplish some of the things that these modern trumpet players have done.

Since Dizzy had learned as a child never to let a beating kill his spirit, he made the best of his situation with the haughty older musicians in Teddy Hill's band. He had developed the knack of telling himself that he was ready for anything; and he nourished and fortified his courage that way. After Paris, he spent four weeks in London and two weeks in Dublin, Ireland; then he went to Manchester, England, and then home to New York.

Returning to New York from the Hill band's tour, Dizzy

proudly wore a new green tweed coat; he was delighted that his pockets had "the mumps," as he liked to call the bulges made by his money. His first stop was Philadelphia, where he went to some parties and gave his mother a good share of his earnings. Then he returned to work with Hill's band in New York. But he hadn't spent the necessary three months in New York before he had gone to Europe with Teddy Hill. The musicians' union, Local 802 of the American Federation of Musicians, wouldn't let him join the union and work regularly with a band until he started the three-month period all over again.

So he had to take odd jobs for single nights or weekends. Because he needed the money so desperately, he took the risk of sneaking out of New York occasionally to play. If anything ever proved to him how profitable it could be to take risks, it was a job he played with an organist in Washington, D.C. The New York local of the union nearly caught him, but Dizzy managed to make the union believe he had gone to Philadelphia to borrow money from his mother. In Washington, at the theater where he played, he noticed a pretty, petite teenage girl dancing in the chorus line. She never lingered around the stage to chat with musicians and other entertainers. Instead of going to clubs or bars after her own performances ended, she sheltered herself in the dressing room or her hotel room. Dizzy became very curious about the small, elusive girl, whose name was Lorraine Willis.

He decided to send her a note and invite her to have a Coca-Cola with him. Lorraine thought he was kidding, because she knew that most musicians were wild types.

Coca-Cola was usually the last thing on their minds. She didn't bother to answer him. Dizzy found out she was dancing at a theater in Baltimore. He followed her there and sent her another note. She sent it back to him. They moved on to New York separately. He made another attempt to reach her, leaving a message with his phone number for her at the Apollo Theatre in Harlem, where she was dancing.

This time, she replied. When he heard her voice, he said, "Well, it's about time you called!"

"Say, man, you're lucky I called you at all," Lorraine said.

It was a typical exchange, tinged with affectionate teasing, between them. The amiable young trumpeter had plenty of self-confidence. He had actually caught her interest with his first note. But Lorraine had great style and self-respect. Always proud of keeping her wits about her, the petite woman with her warm smile and steady gaze would make it her mission to love and take care of Dizzy and protect him from making mistakes. She made sure he made the right business decisions. She didn't let him squander his earnings or get sidetracked by extremes. She noticed everything and had a fabulous memory. Actually, Dizzy himself, though he was hotheaded, had excellent judgment about what his career moves should be. His choice of the warm, loyal Lorraine, who knew how to save his money, was another example of his instinctive astuteness. Lorraine complemented his talents brilliantly, and she respected his devotion to his trumpet, though she liked to complain about all the things he did wrong when he wasn't playing music.

Sometimes the couple's friends were amazed at how critical Lorraine could be when she talked to Dizzy. She portrayed him as foolish, while she was practical. But she could express her opinions with wit and high spirits. Dizzy found her indispensable. Above all, she was a lovely-looking woman, with exquisitely chiseled features; her bright mind and beauty captivated him.

Other musicians thought Dizzy was very lucky to have such a fine, down-to-earth woman. Born, as he had been, in a small South Carolina town, Lorraine had discovered she had the talent to become a dancer. She liked dancing in a sociable group in order to earn the money she needed to take care of herself. A wizard at budgeting, she regularly sent home about half her salary to her mother.

Dizzy and his brother J. P. had moved to another apartment. Then J. P. left without warning; Dizzy, who had almost no income after his trip to Europe, had become a burden. He refused to work as a dishwasher or do anything but play music during the three lean months when the union wouldn't let him take a steady job. Most musicians took menial jobs to survive during those three months. Not daring to leave town to work very often, Dizzy spent most of his time hanging around the Apollo, hoping to catch a glimpse of Lorraine. She was angry with Dizzy's brother for deserting him.

Dizzy had to beg Teddy Hill for fifteen cents for a bowl of soup, but Hill wouldn't let Dizzy draw on the salary he would be earning when he rejoined the band. Instead, Teddy told Dizzy to ask his girlfriend for money. When Lorraine heard that, she became furious with Hill and began feeding Dizzy herself. "I didn't feel sorry for him," she later

Dizzy's father, James Gillespie, and mother, Lotte Powe Gillespie. This photo was taken sometime before 1927 in Cheraw, South Carolina. (in *To BE…or Not to BOP*)

Dizzy and his older brother Wesley (in *To BE ... or Not to BOP*)

Dizzy and Lorraine Gillespie around the time of their wedding in 1940 (in *To BE… or Not to BOP*)

Billy Eckstine with Kenny Clarke and Tommy Potter at Carnegie Hall, December 1948 (Institute of Jazz Studies, Rutgers University)

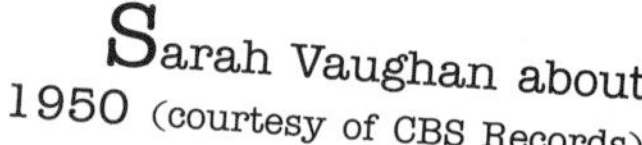

Sarah Vaughan about 1950 (courtesy of CBS Records)

Charlie Parker in 1947 (Institute of Jazz Studies, Rutgers University)

1948: (from the left) Thelonious Monk; Howard McGhee; trumpeter Roy Eldridge, Dizzy's idol; and Teddy Hill (Institute of Jazz Studies, Rutgers University)

Dizzy leads his orchestra, circa 1948 (Institute of Jazz Studies, Rutgers University)

Dizzy on trumpet at Music Inn, Lenox, Massachusetts, mid-1950s (Institute of Jazz Studies, Rutgers University)

Dizzy in the sixties or seventies (Institute of Jazz Studies, Rutgers University)

Dizzy Gillespie in the 1950s after his horn was accidentally bent
(Institute of Jazz Studies, Rutgers University)

recalled for his book, *To BE or Not . . . to BOP*. "I did it the way I was brought up. If I had a roll, and you didn't have anything, I was supposed to give you half of it, whether I wanted to or not."

Lorraine's friends advised her to find a more successful musician for a boyfriend. Actually she didn't want *any* kind of musician for a boyfriend. Often away from home for tours, most musicians did anything they pleased whenever they liked and with whomever they fancied. Lorraine would have to ignore or bury her annoyance with that fact of the musicians' lifestyle. She was a woman who liked to crochet and knit and who liked to read the Bible; she took religion seriously. At the time she met Dizzy, she was sharing a room with several other dancers who were always away, staying with their boyfriends. So Lorraine had the whole room to herself for the quiet life she loved.

She had been married before, when she was a young teenager. Her first husband had died of a brain tumor. Widowed at a young age, Lorraine had been forced to find the courage and strength to go on after facing sorrow. She had no interest in frivolity.

Only one of her girlfriends, also a dancer, urged her to take Dizzy seriously. Her girlfriend thought that Dizzy was a nice young man, really smitten with Lorraine. Even without that encouragement, Lorraine would probably have given her heart to the funny, starving trumpeter. She approved of his driving ambition and belief in his music. Dizzy knew she was saving his life by loving him and giving him money to buy food, and he adored her and never forgot her kindness.

As soon as his waiting period for union membership

ended, Dizzy found more work than he could handle. He played with Teddy Hill, and also with the Savoy Sultans, which was the house band at the Savoy Ballroom, and with Edgar Hayes's band, and with a Latin bandleader who asked Dizzy to play the maracas—a Cuban rhythm instrument made from a gourd—as well as the trumpet. From the Latin bandleader, Dizzy learned the rhythmic basis of all Afro-Cuban music—the clave beat, which goes: one-two, one-two-three, and sometimes one-two-three, one-two. It was an important lesson for Dizzy, who fell madly in love with the exuberant, exotic beat.

In those days the life of musicians was especially hard, and some of them drank to cope with the stress. They had to travel constantly on buses to do one-night stands. They rarely knew from one day to the next if they had jobs. Sometimes club owners and bandleaders didn't keep their promises to pay salaries. The conditions of work could make musicians unstable. Yet Dizzy was always a very reliable employee. Bandleaders could count on him to show up sober and on time for performances. He hated it when other musicians were late. He never made a habit of taking drugs, either, as some musicians did.

Drug dealers went to clubs and gave away drugs free to musicians, and then they started to charge them when they needed more. Some people were tricked into becoming addicts—but not Dizzy.

At that time Dizzy's friendship with drummer Kenny Clarke was becoming closer. Kenny was experimenting with rhythms. Instead of playing the primary rhythm on the bass drums, Clarke kept time on the cymbals and used the bass drums for accents. The technique was called "dropping bombs." He also began playing many rhythms in one song—polyrhythms. Other drummers before Kenny had begun to modernize jazz drumming. Count Basie's drummer had already started using the high hat, the top cymbal of the drum set, for a light sound to accent the swing era's danceable beat. Clarke took the concept further, breaking up the rhythm, making it more diversified. Dizzy was fascinated by Clarke's ideas, and he started showing Clarke new chords on the piano. That inspired Clarke to play even more creative rhythms on the drums, and he in turn gave Dizzy new ideas for harmonies, accents, phrasings, and wild rides all over his trumpet.

Many times Teddy Hill thought about firing Clarke for breaking up the rhythm in the band. Dizzy always talked Hill out of it. Dizzy later said that the most important thing that happened to him in his early period, in 1938 and 1939, was working with Kenny Clarke. Clarke modified the concept of rhythm in jazz from a dance beat into artful accompaniment for soloists. His bold ideas could inspire a whole band.

In 1939 Hill's band stopped playing at the Savoy, and Dizzy had to find other jobs. He and Kenny Clarke kept playing together for Edgar Hayes, whose saxophonist, Rudy Powell, wrote arrangements for the group. One day Dizzy became fascinated with a chord in a Powell arrangement—an E-flat chord built on an A; or the flatted fifth. Dizzy really liked the sound of it. "Damn, listen . . . listen . . . ," he told himself. He began playing it over and over in his solos. It wasn't called a flatted fifth right away; it was considered a half step. No matter what it was called, it became so popular that it symbolized the whole new musical style.

From that note, Dizzy discovered "a lot of pretty notes in a chord," he said, that were good to hold for a while. They added color to his work, he discovered, more so than if he had run over them quickly. Later he would teach the principle to a younger trumpeter, Miles Davis, who wanted to learn all he could from Dizzy.

Others would say that Dizzy may have learned the flatted fifth from Thelonious Monk, a brilliant young composer and pianist, who was then hanging out at Minton's Playhouse in Harlem. He would become a forceful developer of the bebop repertory in the early 1940s. Monk helped Dizzy discover other chords and many other aspects of harmony, and Dizzy repeatedly used the chords Monk showed him. Soon all the young progressives gravitated toward the flatted fifth, saying it led them to invent many lovely musical ideas—phrases, melodies, rhythms, songs.

Edgar Hayes noticed how much Dizzy loved his music; he was always ready to play. If another player in the band didn't come in exactly on time in a piece of music, Dizzy jumped in and started playing that man's solo—not to be mean or greedy, Hayes felt, but because Dizzy didn't want the music to lose momentum. Hayes admired Dizzy and a few other young progressives in his band. They got so hot and loud, so intense and exciting, in the wee hours of the morning in a club where they played on 140th Street in Harlem that the neighbors sent word to shut them up. Even so, Hayes thought he had one of the best bands in New York.

Dizzy's paychecks, though, were irregular and small. And he dreamed about marrying Lorraine. He told her how much he hated to see her dancing at the Apollo, because he knew that dancing was one of the hardest jobs in the world. Many nights Lorraine came home so tired that all she could do was take her clothes off, eat, and fall into bed to get enough rest. She needed the energy to dance again the next day. But Dizzy didn't have enough money to support her, except in his dreams.

Among Lorraine's many friends in show business was Cab Calloway's valet, Rudolph. With her charm and sense of humor, as Dizzy would recount in his memoirs, she told Rudolph, "Please get that nigger a job, because I'm tired. Get Dizzy a job with Cab Calloway." Mario Bauza, a multi-instrumentalist and one of the first Cubans to arrive to play jazz in the United States, was working as lead trumpeter in Cab's band. Mario knew Cab was looking for another trumpet player. So Mario plotted to have Dizzy audition in a way that was sure to excite the bandleader.

Dizzy was sneaked backstage, given a uniform, and put on the bandstand to take Mario's place. Cab didn't know about the switch. One of the other trumpeters was alerted, and he let Dizzy take solos to accompany the dancers as they did their soft-shoe routines. On the night Dizzy auditioned, he noticed the dancers were inspired by his accompaniment, and he hoped that Cab noticed, too. Soon after that, Rudolph telephoned Dizzy and told him to come right away. He was to start with Cab's band that night at the Cotton Club downtown in New York. Dizzy found out that he would earn eighty dollars a week in town, one hundred dollars a week on the road. Cab Calloway's band was the top of the ladder for an African-American, big-band musician. Cab paid excellent salaries, and he traveled in style, sometimes with his own train car, to avoid the insults and inconveniences of segregation.

So Dizzy went to the Victoria Cafe, a little midtown Manhattan club, where he had been playing with Edgar Hayes. He wanted to collect his pay for three nights' work—nineteen dollars—but Hayes refused to give Dizzy the money. "You've got a good job," Hayes said, referring to the Calloway band. Dizzy pulled Hayes's eyeglasses off his face and ran out of the club. When Hayes followed, demanding his glasses, Dizzy said he would exchange them for the money. But Hayes decided to press his luck with a fight. As Dizzy told the story, Hayes punched him. With his hand holding the glasses, Dizzy hit Hayes back. The glasses broke and cut Dizzy's hand so badly that he was covered with blood. The Victoria Cafe's bouncer pulled Dizzy and Hayes apart. Dizzy never got his pay, but he felt satisfied when he broke the glasses, because he hated having anyone take advantage of him. Years later, a reporter named Bob Herbert would comment, "The jazz world was not for the faint of heart."

Rough-and-ready in those days, Dizzy had grown to his full height of about five feet eleven inches. He would almost always look substantial and strong and give the impression of being taller than he was. His hearty appetite kept his face full and his arms muscular. And there was something in his daring and friendly manner that made people respect his presence. He worried about nothing except injuring a part of him that he needed for playing music.

When Dizzy joined Calloway's band, his hand still hurt. But he played his heart out on a Latin-type song called "Cuban Nightmare," with special love for Mario and Lorraine, the helpers who would never be forsaken.

5

dizzy gillespie meets charlie "bird" parker

NO sooner did Cab Calloway hire him than Dizzy was called to play for a recording session with a rising band-leader, drummer and vibraphonist, Lionel Hampton. On one of the tunes, "Hot Mallets," Dizzy played with flair in his exciting, high-note style. It is one of the wonderful early examples of his bright work. He next recorded with Cab Calloway's band in March 1940. Of special note was Dizzy's song, "Picking the Cabbage," which he wrote, arranged, and played with his usual power. He liked to say that he could hear his developing style and his early fascination with Latin rhythms on that song, though most people still primarily heard his legacy from

Roy Eldridge. That was what Cab Calloway wanted for his band. Dizzy's adventures with harmonies still lay ahead of him.

Earning a good salary, Dizzy took Lorraine out of the Apollo chorus line and on the road with him. In Boston, he reminded her of the city's legacy of Puritanism. They were breaking the law by living together as man and wife without having gone through a legal ceremony. He thought they should be married, he told her. Lorraine said, "Okay." They went to a courthouse for the wedding on May 9, 1940. And for many years thereafter, young Mrs. Gillespie, who looked like a little princess, often traveled on the road with Dizzy. Later, after she became plagued by allergies, she preferred to stay home. Dizzy stayed in touch with her all the time by telephone, and he told people his homecomings constituted thousands of honeymoons.

Milt Hinton, Calloway's bassist, reflected on the impact Dizzy had on the band.

> He was about as crazy as you can find, and always like Peck's bad boy, always trying something new. Whether he could do it or whether he couldn't, he was going to make this tremendous attempt at it, and take all kinds of abuses. . . . I was amazed because he knew more, even though I'm older than he is. But he had been more involved in this New York and Philadelphia rat race. And he was very deep into his chord changes and his substitutions which hadn't even hit this band yet, not at all. . . . Anybody making a substitution for a C chord? Nobody ever dreamed of that. If it was a C, you just played it, baby. And that was it.

After Hinton told Dizzy that the new ideas were fascinating, Dizzy started taking him to the roof of the downtown Cotton Club between shows and teaching him the changes. Sometimes Hinton played them correctly; sometimes he missed. When he played the right notes, he turned around and looked for approval from Dizzy. Dizzy made a circle with his thumb and forefinger to signify success. But if Hinton missed the note, Dizzy held his nose, as if he smelled something bad. Many of the other men in the band didn't talk about music with Dizzy. They talked about real estate, paychecks, and security. Dizzy felt so frustrated by their lack of interest in his ideas that he started acting even more mischievous than usual on the bandstand—"eccentric," he called himself.

In 1940 Calloway's band headed for Kansas City for a one-night stand in a theater. When Dizzy stepped off the bus, an old friend, trumpeter Buddy Anderson, greeted him. "Hey, man," he said. "There's a saxophonist you have got to hear. His name is Charlie Parker."

"Saxophonist? A saxophonist?" Dizzy said without much interest. "I've heard all the great saxophonists." He named some great swing era players who jammed in Harlem clubs—among them Coleman Hawkins, who had made a classic recording of "Body and Soul" in 1939; Don Byas, who played with Duke Ellington; and Lester Young, a member of Count Basie's band. "There can't be nothing that I haven't heard among the saxophone players," Dizzy said with his soft southern drawl.

"Yes, you have to hear him," Buddy Anderson insisted.

Dizzy checked into a room at the Booker T. Washington

Hotel, which was segregated for African Americans only. Right away, Buddy Anderson brought Charlie "Bird" Parker, a big man with a deep, quiet, baritone voice, to the room and introduced Bird to Dizzy. Bird took out his saxophone and started playing. His phrasing fascinated the older, more established musician. "I can't believe the way he is playing," Dizzy later wrote. "I've never heard anything like his style before." Dizzy took out his trumpet and began to play, too.

"Bird played the blues like nobody else in the world. As fast as anybody else in the world. Keys didn't make no difference to him. I said, 'Here's the man.' I was completely convinced here was the Jesus of music. We played all day. We forgot to eat." That night, Dizzy would always remember, "I barely got to the job with Cab."

Bird admired Dizzy, too, and would later tell an interviewer, "He was playing as they say in the vernacular in the streets, a boocoo (*beaucoup*) of horn, just like all of the horns packed up in one." Dizzy left town with Cab's band the next day. But he would see Bird a great deal in a couple of years, when they started to experiment together after hours in Minton's and Clark Monroe's Uptown House. Those were the Harlem clubs where, beginning in 1942, the progressives jammed regularly to develop their new style of jazz. That year, too, Bird and Dizzy joined a touring dance band led by an adventurous pianist, Earl "Fatha" Hines. Dizzy and Bird also began to write songs together, and they rushed to show each other the songs they wrote on their own.

Bird played with great naturalness; he didn't seem to

have to plan where his creative instincts took him. He always knew exactly which notes to play and how to play them. Dizzy kept developing his ideas purposefully, through intense deliberation, trial and error, and careful analysis. He learned and adopted the flatted fifth chord, which gave bebop its trademark plaintive sound, while Bird seemed to know all the chord changes instinctively. He, too, had several influences, of course, and he had learned from them by ear. A Texas-born saxophonist, Buster Smith, went to live in Kansas City for a while and influenced Bird when the youngster stood outside a house and listened to Buster in a jam session. Bird listened to his heart for directions about what route to take, what notes to play, and how to phrase his melody lines and embellishments.

One of Dizzy's friends in Calloway's band, Danny Barker, a traditional rhythm-playing guitarist from New Orleans, liked to hear Dizzy at work on chord progressions. Even though Dizzy sometimes started to play lines that he couldn't find a way to finish, and Cab Calloway tried to discourage him, Barker told Dizzy to keep trying the new chords. Barker himself knew he could never play in Dizzy's style, but it fascinated the older musician.

Dizzy kept playing and practicing his unusual, attention-getting notes and doing comedy routines on the bandstand—"nothing foolish," recalled one musician, "but he was always ready to have fun." Because of this he was blamed for everything that went wrong in the band.

One night, during a performance, Milt Hinton missed the chord changes that Dizzy was teaching him. Dizzy held his nose for Hinton to see when he turned around.

Another trumpeter in the band, who also had his mischievous moments, was overcome by a mood that night. At about the same moment Dizzy held his nose, the other trumpeter threw several spitballs at the drummer. One of them veered off course and traveled to the front of the bandstand. It missed Cab, who watched it fly while he was singing.

When the performance was over, Cab started climbing up the bandstand to the trumpet section, heading for Dizzy: "You, Dizzy, you up there throwing spitballs on stage."

Dizzy denied it: "You've got that wrong. I'm not throwing anything on the stage."

As Dizzy later told the story, "Cab jumped into the saxophone section, then to the trombones, and was coming to get me. . . ."

Cab and Dizzy stopped short of a fight on the bandstand, and Cab went off to his dressing room. "And he got to his dressing room, and he saw me passing by," Dizzy continued, "and he came out and he grabbed me by the collar . . . that's the last thing he remembered . . . if you get close enough to me, you've got to get cut."

Milt Hinton saw Cab put a hand on Dizzy's face; it might have been that Cab slapped Dizzy. Then Dizzy stabbed Cab in a buttock. Though smaller than both Dizzy and Cab, Hinton tried to separate them. Some of the bigger musicians in the band came running to stop the fight. Cab's elegant white suit was bloodstained. Hinton heard Cab tell Dizzy right after the fight, "Now you just get your things and get on outta here."

Dizzy went back to his dressing room, where Lorraine was waiting. "She took one look at me and started packing. She thought, 'I'm not going to say anything to this fool!' So Cab paid me and sent me back home. That's how I got out of Cab's band," Dizzy would recount in a soft voice.

"I had a mess," Cab told people whenever he repeated the story. He had to go to the hospital for stitches. Dizzy and Lorraine took a bus back from New Haven, Connecticut, to New York. When they met the Calloway band at its Manhattan hotel, they saw that Cab was all right. Of course, Cab didn't speak to Dizzy.

6

"dizzy dares to be different"

EVENTUALLY Cab found out that another trumpeter had thrown the spitball. Even before then, Cab had begun speaking to Dizzy again. It took them only a few years to mend their relationship. But for a while after the stabbing, some other bandleaders were afraid to hire Dizzy.

First Dizzy played with Ella Fitzgerald's band, which she had inherited from drummer and bandleader Chick Webb. Ella had become a national star with her recording of "A Tisket, a Tasket" with Chick's band. After Chick died of spinal tuberculosis, Ella led the band with a great deal of assistance from the instrumentalists. The band disintegrated when most of the musicians were drafted, some to fight in World War II, some to play in the military bands.

Dizzy managed to convince the draft board to turn him down. His version of the story may have been more a show of bravado than the precise truth. He showed up for induction with only the clothes on his back. He carried his trumpet in a paper bag. By then he was well aware of how strange that looked, and he didn't usually carry the horn that way anymore. But he wanted to make a bad impression. He told the examiners that he didn't need clothes, only his trumpet. When they asked him if he was ready to shoot his German enemies, Dizzy replied that he had nothing against them. He might even mistake an American for a German. In his book, *To BE or Not . . . to BOP*, Dizzy claimed his answers and manner convinced the U.S. Army that he was crazy. Dizzy wore thick glasses for most of his life and had to undergo operations for cataracts on his eyes when he was in his thirties—and later in life, in his seventies, too. His developing eye problems alone could have persuaded the army to leave him alone, if the doctors discovered them. In any case, he was free to work in the bands at home while others went to war.

A much-admired arranger, Walter Gil Fuller, convinced a bandleader, Les Hite, to hire Dizzy, because Dizzy could read music and was one of the best technicians around, with great facility in jazz. Jazz trumpeters, not classical trumpet players, were the pioneers in discovering the capabilities of the instrument. Hite didn't want Dizzy, because of what he had done to Cab Calloway. But Fuller knew that Hite needed Dizzy's spectacular gifts.

Fuller was quickly justified for making sure Dizzy got into the Hite band. On July 14, 1942, a music magazine published a review of four new recordings made by the Les Hite band. The reviewer wrote: "Hite stresses emsembles. Only one solo is distinctive on the four sides, and that's Dizzy Gillespie's trumpet on 'Bounce'—one of the wackiest and [most] daring takeoffs ever recorded. A couple of clinks creep in, too, but at least Dizzy dares to be different. Nothing exciting aside from Dizzy's display. Just good big band stuff. . . ."

Sometimes when bandleaders wanted to fire a man, they fired the whole band, then hired back everyone except the person they had wanted to fire. This avoided complications with unions and musicians. That's what Les Hite did when Dizzy began arguing with Hite's drummer about what Dizzy wanted the drummer to play. Dizzy didn't like the drummer's heavy-handed, old-fashioned style on the bass drum solos, and one night Dizzy stopped playing in the middle of a solo. Hite had never gotten over his fear of Dizzy and had always communicated with him by passing messages through Fuller. Now Hite fired the whole band. Then he immediately hired back everyone except Dizzy.

Dizzy found work as a sideman irregularly. He played with Coleman Hawkins briefly on Manhattan's Fifty-second Street. They quibbled about money, because Dizzy wanted a few dollars above union scale. "Hawk," as Hawkins was called, couldn't pay the bonus. Then alto saxophonist Benny Carter hired Dizzy and took him into Kelly's Stable and the Famous Door, two of the hot Fifty-second Street clubs of the era. The street had many little jazz clubs, and some of the most exciting players in the world liked to perform in them. Fifty-second Street was eventually honored with a plaque memorializing it as "Swing Street." Carter, who was also a trumpeter, an arranger, and a composer as well as bandleader, defended Dizzy's unusual style when audiences found it difficult to listen to the brash flights and wanted to know what he was playing. Carter had worked in a prestigious British radio band until World War II started. Because of all his experience, Carter thought the new music was so interesting that he wanted to give Dizzy the chance to show it off.

Lucky Millinder, a bandleader who couldn't play any instrument or even read a note, hired Dizzy. This time Dizzy actually got to perform with the organization. Lucky knew every note of every song, every instrument's part, by heart. "Two bars before you're coming in, Lucky's waving his hand, getting you ready," Dizzy noted. "And then you'd put your horn up there, and he'd bring you in, understand—on that beat—wherever that beat was. Sometimes that beat would be on the second note of a triplet, and he'd bring you in. Yeah. . . . He was great!"

Dizzy was proud of a riff—a musical phrase—that he played in a recording of "Little John Special" done with the Millinder band. The riff was a three-note phrase with a big interval jump—a leap from a low register to a high one and back down to a low one. The phrase was plaintive, intense, and jubilant all at once. It soon became the basis for one of his best-known compositions, "Salt Peanuts," which he wrote in 1942. Dizzy had actually used the riff, or lick—the words meant the same thing in musicians' slang—even before he played it on "Little John Special."

"Salt Peanuts," a composition that developed from the

intriguingly off-kilter phrase, became very popular with progressive musicians. Everybody played it. Aspiring musicians fell in love with it. Dizzy had forfeited the salary from the Calloway band, but the years after he left Calloway were a very fertile, exciting time. He wrote many of his greatest songs in the early 1940s. First came "A Night in Tunisia," then "Salt Peanuts," which he wrote with Bird. And Dizzy's arrangements for compositions by jazz pianist Thelonious Monk and Broadway songwriter Jerome Kern became integral parts of the songs.

He spent hours working with Monk, who played with drummer Kenny Clarke in the band at Minton's Playhouse in Harlem in 1942. Monk taught Dizzy invaluable lessons about harmonies. Dizzy would recall, "I could always find chords on the piano, and people helped me. . . . I'll never forget the day that Monk showed me a . . . chord . . . that opened up new avenues. I had never heard of that chord before . . . I used it on [the arrangement of] Monk's tune, 'Round Midnight,' and on many others, on 'Woody 'n' You,' . . . I used that particular chord. . . . Everytime I'd write something, that chord would be there someplace—for the resolving someplace."

Most audiences and music critics still resisted bebop's odd sounds and said they consisted of wrong notes. Actually, to play bebop, the young players needed a well-defined rhythmic sense, a knowledge of harmony, and virtuoso abilities on their instruments. Just starting to weather the critical storm in the early 1940s, Dizzy and Bird jammed together in Harlem, working with Monk and Kenny Clarke, two of the most important experimenters.

Soon a young drummer named Max Roach and others joined the group. Anyone who was interested and able to play fast and well enough was welcomed. Of the older musicians, tenor saxophonist Coleman Hawkins was a firm supporter of the beboppers. He had spent the 1930s in Europe and had hoped to come back to the United States and find progress being made in jazz. But his old friends were playing exactly the same way they had done when he had left. The young progressives were taking an interesting new direction, he thought. So he liked to jam with them at Minton's.

The clique of experimenters met at Dizzy's tiny apartment, at 2040 Seventh Avenue, in the middle of Harlem, where Lorraine cooked for them. Then Dizzy and his friends could walk outside and find many places featuring music at all hours of the day and night. Lorraine enjoyed helping them out with meals and hospitality. She had a sense of humor, and she didn't want Dizzy to become too impressed with himself or his friends, so she teased them all on occasion. She particularly poked fun at Charlie Parker.

7

bird

CHARLIE PARKER had once been traveling on the road with a group of musicians when their car hit a chicken crossing the highway. He insisted on going back to get the chicken, and carried it to a woman who owned a boardinghouse in a town where the band was going to play. After she cooked the chicken for the musicians, they gave Parker the nickname "Yardbird."

Dizzy called him "Yardbird" and "Yard." Every one else called him "Bird," except for Lorraine, who decided to call him "Yard Dog." At the same time, she admitted, "Bird was a quiet, gentlemanly man. The only thing wrong with him was that habit." In her heart, she felt sorry that he had such a great misfortune. Bird had become a heroin addict as a young teenager, too young to be responsible for his actions. Lorraine noticed that no matter what Dizzy said or how he tried to help his friend to stop taking heroin, Bird couldn't quit. Dizzy told people that he wished he could take Bird into his apartment and force him to get well, but Dizzy was struggling to make a living and establish a career. Music was his center, and Lorraine was his bulwark. He didn't have the time or money to spend nursing Bird. And Bird was stubborn about going his own way.

Bird's problem may have begun with a hospital stay. He had broken some bones in an auto accident as a teenager and had been treated with morphine to ease the pain. When he got out of the hospital, he kept looking for drugs to help relieve the continuing pain. He also wanted to maintain the "high" feeling he had come to like and crave. Nobody in the music world knew Bird before he was a heroin addict.

Bird had begun playing professionally when he was about sixteen years old. Bandleader Jay McShann tolerated Bird's habit and all his strange personality traits because he could play so well. But he fell asleep on the bandstand, and he didn't show up on time for jobs. Sometimes he didn't show up for days. He often pawned his horn to get money for drugs. He was the most aggravating genius one could imagine.

Lorraine and Dizzy kept their home and family life intact and remote from the problems that haunted others. Dizzy never used heroin. Compared to some other musicians, he drank very little alcohol, and he never made a habit of drugs. Lorraine was outspoken against bad habits. Dizzy often told his friends that he steered clear of vices because of her influence.

Bird sometimes showed up at Dizzy's door in the middle of the night. He wanted to play his new songs and have Dizzy write them down. Dizzy made Parker stand in the hall and play, while Dizzy transcribed the notes onto paper. Lorraine didn't want musicians barging into the apartment at all hours of the night.

When he had first heard Charlie Parker, Dizzy had known that they were experimenting along the same lines. Eventually, nearly everyone else would become intrigued with Bird's music—"the way he got from one note to the next," as Dizzy summed up Bird's heady style. Like Dizzy, Bird was iconoclastic. That is, he took apart the principles upon which the swing era had thrived, and he made music more exotic, surprising, and expressive, and less predictable.

In some ways, Bird's odyssey had been stranger than Dizzy's. In his midteens, he was laughed off a stage in his native Kansas City for his awkward attempts to play his new, difficult style. He felt humiliated, but he didn't give up. He went to a small town to practice—to "woodshed," as musicians called it. After a few months, he went back to play with Jay McShann's band in Kansas City. McShann loved Bird's style. But Bird felt the need to visit New York City for a while to hear the music being played there. He had married very young and had taken his wife and son to live in the Parker family home with himself and his mother. But soon Bird asked his wife to set him free. He told her he felt that he could become a great musician if she would let him go. She agreed to divorce him. He asked his mother to look after her and the child. Then he went to New York and worked as a dishwasher in Clark Monroe's Uptown House in Harlem.

At Monroe's, where musicians played late at night, Bird jammed for no pay in the wee hours of the morning. According to legend, it was in Clark Monroe's that Bird gave birth to bebop. Of course the tale is too simple, for many people were paving the way for bebop's development in the 1930s and 1940s. But one night, while playing a solo above the chords of "Cherokee," the Ray Noble tune popular at that time, Bird went further afield from the written melody than any jazz player had ever done before. In fact, his improvisation turned into a separate tune that became known as "Ko Ko." It was then that Bird realized he could create an entirely new repertory based upon the chords of older songs.

He returned to Kansas City and played with McShann for a while again. Eventually he went back to New York City, where he lived a double life. He played music with friends such as Dizzy and kept company with drug pushers and addicts. Some of the addicts were musicians who actually started using drugs because they admired Bird's style so much. They thought heroin would help them to play like Bird. He kept warning them that it would only hurt them. They didn't believe him, because he was playing at the top of his powers despite the drugs.

Kenny Clarke, the drummer, was developing the rhythmic principles of bebop. Oscar Pettiford, a bass player, was sufficiently inventive, strong, and adventurous to play bebop's new sound. The bassist took over the basic beat, freeing the drummer and the guitarist (if there was one in a group), to play creatively. The bassist also played solos, with improvisations. Dizzy served as a focal point for all the musicians. Analyzing his role, he thought his main contributions were harmonic and rhythmic—experimenting with chords and blending Afro-American and Latin rhythms. He taught what he knew to many piano players and other instrumentalists.

Minton's was a sort of paradise for Dizzy, Bird, and all the progressives. There Dizzy met every musician he needed to know, and he developed the new style with them—"our music," as he started calling it protectively and proudly. And on Monday nights, entertainers from the Apollo Theatre showed up to enjoy the jam sessions and eat the free food provided by Minton's owners. So the bebop style went on display. Nobody stopped the musicians from jamming at Minton's, because the management was connected to the union. Though it was against union rules to play or jam without payment, nobody was fined for playing at Minton's jam sessions. Musicians liked—and needed—to jam for practice to improve their technique.

Few white musicians went to Minton's to play bebop, but the handful who did could play very well. Those who couldn't keep up, African Americans or whites, were forced off the bandstand. The bebop clique launched into some outrageously complex figures when they heard a weak player in their midst, and so moved him out quickly.

Dizzy went to Minton's when he wasn't working downtown on Fifty-second Street, "Swing Street," for pay. Usually he was free only on Mondays. After hours he went to Clark Monroe's Uptown House, where musicians also could eat for no charge and play until the sun came up. Bird was playing there again, too, in the early 1940s.

Dizzy recalled the days:

> What we were doing at Minton's was playing seriously, creating a new dialogue among ourselves, blending our ideas into a new style of music. You only have so many notes, and what makes a style is how you get from one note to the other. We had some fundamental background training in European harmony and music theory superimposed on our own knowledge from Afro-American musical tradition. We invented our own way of getting from one place to the next. I taught myself chords on the piano beginning at Laurinburg because I could hear chords in European music without anybody telling me what they were. Our phrases were different. . . . Musically, we were changing the way that we spoke, to reflect the way that we felt. New phrasing came in with the new accent. Our music had a new accent.

At another time he recalled, for a book written by swing era authority Stanley Dance about popular bandleader Earl Hines, that "Charlie Parker's playing took on a decided change after he met me, and my playing took on a decided change after I met him. . . . That's the way it was. . . . [We had] a mutual non-aggression pact . . . mutual respect for one another. We inspired each other."

8

traveling with the big bands

DIZZY'S fervent commitment to developing progressive music at that time didn't make him a rich man. He was regarded as just another young sideman by the established bandleaders. They had their quirks and eccentricities, in Dizzy's view. One, Lucky Millinder, was known to fire musicians, then hire them back at higher salaries. Dizzy was hired by Millinder in the early 1940s, and eventually Dizzy's time came to be fired by him. Millinder added to the excitement by spreading a rumor that Dizzy was "losing his chops"—musicians' slang meaning he was losing his ability to play well. That made Dizzy angry, and when Millinder tried to hire Dizzy back, just before the firing was to become final, Dizzy said no. He had another job lined up.

He traveled to Philadelphia and found a job in a little club called the Down Beat. Some of the young white players who would become bebop disciples used to go there to hear Dizzy. One night, singer Billy Eckstine and drummer Shadow Wilson were passing through Philadelphia. They were playing with Earl Hines's band, and after work they slipped into the Down Beat, listened to Dizzy, and said, "Man, you come over here to Earl Hines." Dizzy was reluctant to leave the Down Beat. But the Hines job had prestige. So in 1942, Dizzy went on the road again with a big band, this time led by the well-known, popular pianist, Hines.

Hines was clever enough to know he should have at least a modest amount of that new music sound that everyone was beginning to talk about. "Amongst all of the younger musicians, bebop was *the* thing in New York," Dizzy later said. So Hines didn't squelch Dizzy's creativity. Earl soon hired Charlie Parker, too. Earl himself had heard Bird playing with a band in Detroit and had been quite impressed. Later, when Bird was jamming at Clark Monroe's Uptown House in Harlem in 1943, getting his meals free, and looking for work, Hines stopped in. He needed a tenor player at the time, and Bird said he could play tenor. So Hines bought him a horn. Bird was still technically working for Kansas City bandleader Jay McShann. Hines went to McShann, a jovial, soulful, round-faced man with a superb piano style, and asked if he could buy Bird's contract. McShann sold it to Hines for the money that Parker owed him.

In Earl's band, Bird remained his exquisitely unreliable self. Once he was almost fired, but Hines made Bird promise that he would definitely be better about showing up for work. Bird went to sleep under the bandstand to be sure to be at the theater on time for the next show; then he slept through it. When Hines saw Jay McShann again, Hines complained about how sorry he was to have hired Bird, saying that half the time Bird's horn was in a pawnshop to raise money for drugs. McShann was quite amused by Hines's plight, since Hines had bargained hard to entice Bird away.

Hines had become well known in jazz circles when he was working with Louis Armstrong and when he was leading his own band at the Grand Terrace in Chicago. Broadcasting from that club, he had become an influence on many youngsters. Hines took his band all over the North and South playing for dances, which usually paid him well. The young musicians in his band in 1942 and 1943 weren't stars yet, but their special fire appealed to him and to audiences.

The band never recorded that year because the musicians' union called a strike against recording companies in order to get better working conditions for musicians. But people who heard the band in live performances thought it was excellent. And all his life Dizzy would remember incidents in the band that helped forge his close friendship and collaboration with Bird.

On the road with Earl, during an intermission at a whites-only dance in Pine Bluff, Arkansas, Dizzy sat down to play the piano. "A guy walked up to me and thumped a penny, or a nickel, or a dime on the piano" and asked for a corny song, Dizzy recalled. Dizzy pushed the coin away and kept trying to work on his chords.

After the dance, everyone was packing up the instruments. Dizzy had to go to the bathroom. Thinking that all the customers had left, he went to the men's room designated exclusively for whites. When he came out, the man who had requested the corny song hit him over the head. Dizzy saw he had blood all over his uniform. He went to grab something to fight back, but the men in the band stopped him. "And Charlie Parker came up and said to the man, 'You took advantage of my friend, you cur.' " In retelling the story through the years, Dizzy always explained, "A cur is a dog. In English. It was the first time I ever heard that word."

In the band, along with Dizzy and Bird, were more future bebop stars and followers, and two fine singers, Billy Eckstine and Sarah Vaughan. Hines hired nineteen-year-old Sarah in April 1943, just after she had won an Apollo Theatre amateur night contest. She and Eckstine sang duets in the band. Sarah loved the music that Dizzy and Bird and a few others in the band were working to develop. And Dizzy noticed Sarah's reverence for Bird: "She didn't want to know about nothing but Bird's music."

Dizzy wrote several arrangements while in the Hines band. Hines liked to say that he himself gave the title to one of Dizzy's original compositions, "A Night in Tunisia." Though one of Dizzy's very early songs, it would become his most famous. Dizzy later explained many times how he had been sitting at a piano one day. "And after hitting this chord, a D minor, I said to myself, 'boy, that's a nice chord change.' And the melodic line of 'A Night in Tunisia' was in that chord. . . . I had to write a bridge for it, of course, and I didn't have a name for it." Hines claimed that he thought of the name because Tunisia, in Africa, was an area of fighting during World War II and on everybody's mind. But Dizzy would recall that someone else, though he couldn't remember exactly who, had named the tune before he had ever played in the Hines band. Dizzy said the bridge was a reflection of the chord that Thelonious Monk had showed him in a jam session in Harlem. Then Dizzy added a Latin rhythm.

By the end of 1943, the youngsters in Hines's band refused to bide their time anymore. Hines had given them a lot of leeway, but it still wasn't enough for them. Dizzy had written a beautiful arrangement for Sarah of "East of the Sun, West of the Moon," but it was a bit too minor in feeling, and rather slow for dancing—too different for Earl to want to feature with his band.

Dizzy soon became one of the young musicians most eager to break free and find more opportunities to show off his work. He kept trying to convince Billy Eckstine to start a band to feature the new music.

Since Eckstine already had many fans, he was the logical choice for the bandleader. The Hines band owed a great deal of its popularity to Eckstine, a very handsome man blessed with a magnificent, rich baritone and a seductive, elegant way of phrasing lines and pronouncing words. Through the 1930s and 1940s, his voice kept deepening, and he developed a vibrato which would help make him an internationally famous ballad singer in the 1950s.

Dizzy, Eckstine, Bird, and other young progressives left

the Hines band with the idea that they would try to work together again in the near future in a band led by Eckstine. Eckstine went to play on Swing Street for a while. But as a single act, he didn't have the success that he had hoped for. His manager, Billy Shaw, decided that Billy Eckstine should form his own band.

At the time, Dizzy was having even less success than Eckstine. Few people knew who Dizzy was. He got a job playing with the Duke Ellington band for a few weeks simply because Ellington needed a musician to fill in for a while. (Later, in the 1950s, after he became a star, Dizzy would record "Upper Manhattan Medical Group" with Duke.) So when Billy Eckstine asked Dizzy if he would like to become the musical director of the new band, Dizzy was thrilled. Billy Shaw didn't like the idea, because he didn't like Dizzy's music. Eckstine insisted that the band would be great. Shaw spoke to Dizzy and told him to watch his step, behave, promote Eckstine, and, if all went well, Shaw and his son, Milt, also a manager, would help Dizzy put together his own band one day.

Eckstine started lining up the rest of the personnel for the band. He went to Chicago for some, including Bird, who was playing at the Rhumboogie, a club on the South Side, Chicago's African-American ghetto. Eckstine especially wanted him for the new band. Many fine young players would pass through the group.

Wherever the band went it attracted audiences, because of Billy's singing first and foremost. Then people noticed how exciting, fresh, and different the instrumentalists were, too. While Dizzy was its musical director, he wrote an arrangement for a song called "Good Jelly Blues," which he always thought was one of his best. It was a sequel to Eckstine's great hit with Hines, called "Jelly Jelly."

The band had organizational problems. Some musicians were drug users, and they didn't always show up on time for performances. Once, the whole saxophone section was absent from the bandstand. Dizzy himself once missed a performance in Baltimore simply because he slept through his stop on a train from New York and ended up in Washington, D.C. But the band had pizzazz and electricity.

Arranger Walter Gil Fuller, who would begin to work closely with Dizzy in 1945, recalled a performance at the Brooklyn Armory. Jimmie Lunceford's swing era band was playing on one side. Billy's band stood on the other side. "And that was the night that I knew that the whole thing had turned around," Fuller said in Dizzy's book, *To BE or Not . . . to BOP*. "When Billy Eckstine's band was playing, everybody ran around to that side. And you could see the whole crowd moving, shifting around. After a while, the shift stopped. The people stopped going back around to Lunceford's side and stayed on this side with Billy Eckstine. Diz was *the* musical director, right then and there. So that was the first time I got the inkling that the real change had taken place . . . that was the first night that we knew."

Eckstine would always be sentimental about the seven or eight months that Dizzy spent as the musical director. Billy loved the style that Dizzy and Bird brought to the band. Sometimes people thought they were listening to one horn, and it would be Bird and Diz playing together. They had an uncanny ability to play in unison. Also, Bird could play something, and Dizzy could come in and improvise on Bird's idea, and then Bird could take an idea from Dizzy's work and embellish it. If their tones weren't always perfect (and sometimes there was even squeaky playing at their breakneck speeds), their feeling and ideas were always fascinating. Their spiritual connection through music was enormous.

Dizzy shelved none of his comedy. "I'd be out on the stage singing," Billy Eckstine would recall, "and I used to notice people laughing. . . . And then I'd turn around and look back at Diz, and he's just looking straight ahead. Well, all the time that I'm singing, he's doing pantomime to the audience—pointing at me, saying that my teeth are false. . . . And when I'd turn around and look, he's just looking straight up in the air . . . we had a million laughs. Diz is my baby, I love him." Eckstine would be grateful for Dizzy's teaching, too. At any time, no matter what Dizzy was playing, Eckstine could stop him and ask, "What was that?" and Dizzy always explained.

All the musicians with whom Dizzy came into contact had the same experience. He always had time to sit down at the piano and explain anything he was doing. He was never too proud, self-important, or busy. Mary Lou Williams, a popular jazz pianist in Harlem in those days, saw Dizzy coach youngsters in the clubs where he was nurturing bebop. They went on to become stars in studios and the film industry. Mary Lou thought they should send money back to Dizzy regularly, since he had given them the lessons that had helped them succeed. They never did send money, and of course Dizzy never thought about it.

Bob Redcross, a road manager and the person who would make the first recordings of Dizzy and Bird playing together, recalled seeing Dizzy teaching principles of progressive jazz to Art Blakey, the drummer in Eckstine's band. "Diz would get up outta his chair and go put his head right near Blakey's bass drum and stand right down in front of him and be going, 'ooo-bop-she-dow-ooo-bop-bop,' hollering out licks . . . and accents for him to play."

Bird, too, was a great teacher, primarily by his example. A big, gentle man, he was always revered by other musicians, no matter where he went. If they saw him walk into a club where they were playing, they became so flustered that it was difficult for them to keep playing. Bird was barely recognized by the general public, but big band saxophonists, and all the other jazz and pop instrumentalists, and singers, too, worshiped him. In Billy Eckstine's band, the reed section was so in awe of Bird, Bob Redcross recalled, that it sometimes stopped playing to listen to him. "They'd be playing passages and Bird would run into something that'd scare everybody to death," Bob Redcross said.

> And the same thing would happen with Diz. Diz would be playing, man, and the brass section would damn near quit. . . . Diz and Bird . . . would feed each other ideas. I'd hear Diz run across an idea, maybe they were playing solos, running across a passage, and you'd hear Bird maybe later on come up with another treatment of that same passage, taking it somewhere else where it would fit. . . . And another thing about Diz . . . Diz was never envious. Like, he could see someone who had limitations. Somebody else would say,

> "Man, that cat can't play!" "No, man, don't say that because he's got some beautiful ideas," Diz would say. . . . Bird was the same way. If you were sincere in doing what you did and did it to the best of your ability, and said something, he would recognize it and encourage it.

The critics said that Billy Eckstine's band had a muddy sound and played out of tune, because of the innovative harmonies. Dizzy himself never recorded in a studio with Eckstine's organization. Throughout his time as musical director until the end of 1943, the recording ban was in effect. He would always regret that. For the rest of his life, he would recall that the band had sounded wonderful. "I have dreams about that band," he said forty-three years later during a Columbia University radio broadcast celebrating his seventieth birthday.

Dizzy left Billy's band to pursue his own career as a leader, heading for the hurly-burly of Fifty-second Street, Swing Street, in 1944.

9

bebop's debut on swing street

DIZZY won the New Star award from *Esquire* magazine's jazz poll that year. Bassist Oscar Pettiford won the magazine's Gold Star award. They were asked to form a group and play in the Onyx Club on Fifty-second Street. Dizzy found himself in the company of singer Billie Holiday, another *Esquire* Gold Star winner that year, who was singing at the Onyx. He felt encouraged.

To put the sound of bebop across, Pettiford, who had a strong sound anyway, was aided by new, modern amplification equipment. The public loved the little group. Since Kenny Clarke was serving in the army, Max Roach played drums. And George Wallington, a white man, was the pianist. Other bandleaders, black and white, might discriminate against hiring someone because of his race, but Dizzy never did.

Dizzy had wanted Bird for the group to make it a quintet, but Bird had gone home to Kansas City for a while. He didn't answer Dizzy's telegram to come to work. Later Bird said that he had never received it. In the meantime, Don Byas, a smooth, artistic tenor saxophone player and a star of the swing era, heard Dizzy's quartet. Byas was playing in the same club, and he started to sit in with the group because he liked it so much. Soon he switched and made Dizzy's group a quintet. Dizzy loved Don's playing—when Don wasn't drunk. When he was drunk and messing up the music, Dizzy threatened him right on the bandstand.

To play as co-leader of the first bebop group on Fifty-second Street was great exposure for Dizzy. Nobody knew exactly who had first named it, but one critic called the new music "bebop" in honor of the musical nonsense syllables that the progressives were using to sing their songs to one another. Then journalists started calling it "bebop" in print. So Dizzy wrote a tune called "Bebop" in honor of the attention his music was getting. Bird and Max Roach worried that the catchy name "bebop" trivialized the modern music. They wished that the critics just called it music. But the media invention became the formal name. Dizzy thought the abstract syllables were ideal lyrics for "our music," he said. The vowel sounds communicated the feeling that Dizzy wanted the notes to have, because of their register and the many ways they could be played. The sound "eeeee," for example, was excellent for a high note.

Musicians often lived and worked in dingy clubs and

bars in rough neighborhoods. By daylight, even the Fifty-second Street clubs were barren and depressing looking, lit by naked lightbulbs, devoid of any decoration. Some of the Harlem clubs were far more luxurious than the Fifty-second Street joints, which came alive only at night because of the lights, the music, and the crowds. Jazz concerts rarely took place in illustrious concert halls in those days. Musicians performed in all too many "upholstered sewers," as they called some clubs.

Dizzy knew that this was living on the edge, and he might have to protect and defend himself personally as a man, an African-American man, and an artistic, daring trumpeter. He always carried a knife, even if it was only a tiny one hidden in a rabbit's foot. He sometimes was in physical danger, and he liked to be prepared.

One night after Dizzy finished work at the Onyx Club, he and Oscar Pettiford, who was drunk, were talking to a very light-skinned African-American singer named Bricktop on a street corner. Three southern-born sailors asked how Dizzy and Oscar dared to talk to a white woman. Oscar tried to hit a sailor and fell down. That started a fight. Dizzy pushed Oscar into a taxi and tried to get the driver to go to Harlem, but the driver wouldn't budge. Dizzy and Oscar got out and ran into a subway station. The sailors chased them. Since Oscar was so drunk and helpless, Dizzy pushed him through a turnstile. Dizzy stayed behind and pulled his knife on the sailors. When they saw it shining, they swatted it with their coats until he dropped it. One sailor tried to tackle him, and Dizzy hit him over the head with the trumpet in its bag.

"And when I hit him with the trumpet, all these other

sailors were pummeling on my back," Dizzy recalled in his book.

> Boy, they were pummeling me. And I was trying to protect my mouth, running with my hand over it, and they were beating me. . . . Finally I broke through them. . . . I jumped over that little fence at the end of the platform. I ran along that little catwalk there on the side where the workmen walk. I ran up in there and hid, and it was very dark in there. There was only a little space, only about two feet wide. Well, if anybody had come behind me, they had to come one at a time because the rest of it was the third rail. I was standing there, waiting with my horn. . . . I was gonna knock one out and throw him on the tracks, knock another one out and go ahead. But the Shore Patrol came and got them.

Anything could happen to him in those days. It wasn't until 1968 that jazz musicians began to receive recognition as serious artists, with government grants and safe harbor in prestigious music schools.

Dizzy had been playing at the Onyx Club on Swing Street when a pianist brought the famous white bandleader Jimmy Dorsey to hear him. Dorsey was leading a band about ten blocks away at the Hotel Astor near the Paramount Theatre in Times Square. After the show, Dorsey invited Dizzy to go along to a party in a hotel. Dizzy recalled a conversation they had as they walked down the street together.

"Man, you play beautiful," Dorsey said, "but you're black. Suppose you had been white."

Dizzy answered, "Well, if I had been white, I wouldn't have been playing like this. My whole background would have been someplace else."

Dizzy knew that Dorsey didn't have any African-American players in his band. Few white bandleaders did. Though some white bandleaders wanted to hire African-American musicians, the Jim Crow segregation of hotels and restaurants at that time usually made the idea too difficult to put into practice. But Dorsey hired Dizzy to write arrangements behind the scenes, where his race couldn't cause trouble. There were young musicians in all the bands who wanted to play some of that new music. Dizzy put his bebop phrases into an arrangement called "Grand Central Getaway" for Dorsey.

In the 1940s Dizzy also wrote for Ina Ray Hutton's band, for Woody Herman's, for Boyd Raeburn's, and, of course, for Billy Eckstine's. For the opening of "Good Jelly Blues" for Eckstine, Dizzy used one of his favorite bebop lines, and he did it again almost note for note for an arrangement of Jerome Kern's song, "All the Things You Are." He also introduced something new with "Good Jelly Blues"—the double-up arrangement, in which the rhythm section played in one tempo while the horn section played twice as fast. Dizzy used that technique for "I Stay in the Mood for You" for Eckstine's band, too. Though the recording strike was still on, he was able to hear himself play in a radio air check of the Eckstine band that included these songs.

Although Dizzy wrote for white bands that had to discriminate against hiring him to play, he didn't sell his arrangements cheaply. Once, he wrote an arrangement for the clarinetist, Woody Herman, a dear friend and a white man. Dizzy went to get paid by Woody's lawyer in the RKO Building in midtown Manhattan. The lawyer told Dizzy,

> "We rehearsed the music, and how much will it cost?"
> Dizzy replied, "One hundred dollars."
> The lawyer exclaimed, "One hundred dollars!"
> Dizzy said, "Pass me my music, please."
> The lawyer said, "No . . ."
> Dizzy said, "I said that's it."

And they paid him, though it was unheard of to pay one hundred dollars for an arrangement then. Most arrangers were earning half that or even less. Dizzy never said that his writing was superior to everyone else's. But he knew that he was writing music with a fresh sound—the different notes and new phrasing that the bandleaders really wanted to try. "In the music of the forties, our creativity was at our highest point, with Bird and Monk," he later commented. "They represented the age of World War II."

Woody Herman, for whom Dizzy wrote "Woody 'n' You," loved Dizzy's writing so much that he advised Dizzy to quit playing and concentrate on writing music. "What do you want with the trumpet when you write like that?" Woody said. Dizzy could have earned a lot of money as an arranger, but he loved playing too much to take Woody's advice. Dizzy wrote arrangements on the side primarily because he needed the money. "Being hungry will cure you of all moments when you want to relax instead of work," he later observed.

Dizzy also composed "Disorder at the Border" for Coleman Hawkins's band, a group that embraced bebop innovations. Hawk hired pianist Thelonious Monk for the band in 1944. At the time, the critics were making fun of Monk because he wrote and played such odd harmonies in angular, spiky, hesitating rhythms. More than a decade would pass before Monk's distinctive music became critically admired. His shy, odd, quiet personality didn't help promote it, either. Dizzy's piano style came directly from Monk's.

Dizzy both wrote and played for the band that Hawkins led in 1944. Dizzy had clearly become more harmonically daring and polished. His style had expanded way beyond his earlier Roy Eldridge ideal. When Hawkins recorded with Dizzy in the band in February 1944, the sessions were considered by some people to be the first commercial bebop recordings.

A musician finally persuaded Leonard Feather, a rising young jazz writer, pianist, composer, and record producer, to listen to and write about Dizzy. Dizzy and Leonard used to meet on "The Street," as they called Fifty-second Street. Dizzy gave Leonard a tape of Sarah Vaughan singing. Then Feather urged a friend to record Sarah, with Dizzy playing in the accompanying group on the last day of 1944. Dizzy played both trumpet and piano on "A Night in Tunisia," one of the recordings made that day. Feather's budget for the recording session was so small that he assigned himself the job of playing piano. But he wasn't equal to playing Dizzy's song.

By the middle of 1945, Leonard had set up another recording date for Sarah, this time with both Dizzy and Bird playing accompaniment, again for a small company, Guild. Dizzy was leading his own groups, and Bird was back in town, playing in them. Sarah sang "Lover Man" in the studio with Dizzy's quintet, which also played at the Three Deuces on Fifty-second Street. Then in November, Charlie Parker led a sextet on another landmark recording, with Dizzy playing trumpet and piano, and Miles Davis as trumpeter when Dizzy played piano. They played pure bebop songs and arrangements. Leonard Feather became more and more enthusiastic, one of the first jazz critics to support bebop.

The bebop recordings circulated throughout the country and spread the word of the style's arrival and importance to many cities where young musicians, who were trying to learn to play well enough to start careers, listened to them. Bebop excited them. In Los Angeles a jazz club owner named Billy Berg heard the records. He began to be intrigued, even though he was really a swing era jazz fan. He would soon send for the young beboppers to come to California for the first time.

They were still struggling financially. Dizzy's recording career was in a fledgling stage in 1944 and 1945. His playing career in the clubs had its ups and downs. While playing at the Onyx Club on Fifty-second in 1944, Oscar Pettiford, a heavy drinker, often irritated Dizzy. It would become a legend in the jazz world that one should not awaken Pettiford if he had gone to sleep drunk, because he would wake up in a bad mood, ready for a fight.

One night, when Oscar was drunk on the bandstand, Dizzy told him he was a prima donna. Pettiford got angry and threatened to leave. Dizzy said that would be fine. "May you feel the doorknob in your back," were his precise words.

Dizzy left the Onyx Club and formed a group with tenor saxophone player Budd Johnson to play across the street at the Downbeat. Oscar Pettiford hired a trumpet player to replace Dizzy at the Onyx. Despite all the tension behind the scenes, Dizzy was happy to see that there were now two bebop groups on Fifty-second Street.

Drummer Max Roach crossed the street from the Onyx, leaving Pettiford and following Dizzy's lead. Dizzy stayed busy all the time, playing at Kelly's Stable, which was also on "The Street," and in a Greenwich Village club, earning a few more dollars a week in his spare time. He kept spreading the word, teaching other musicians the chords for the progressive style when he jammed in after-hours clubs in Harlem.

The widow of a musician who lived downstairs from Lorraine and Dizzy in Harlem told Dizzy that he could have her family's piano. Dizzy was thrilled to haul it upstairs. It helped him with teaching in his apartment, which, he was proud to note, still functioned as a training center.

He was also pleased about his first big band, the Hepsations of 1945, which his manager, Billy Shaw, and his son, Milt, decided to help him organize. The Shaws paid for it, too, hiring bebop musicians and popular acts. They arranged a tour and sent the band down south, where audiences showed up, hoping to dance and hear the blues.

They hated Dizzy's fast, unusual music. The result was a financial disaster, a professional embarrassment, and a personal disappointment for Dizzy. It was his first truly staggering failure. The band fell apart.

But Dizzy refused to let the failure stop him. Back in New York, he immediately organized a little band that went into the Three Deuces on Fifty-second Street. They had an appreciative audience. Dizzy was thrilled by the way he and Yard communicated on the bandstand. "Shaw Nuff," one of the songs they recorded for the little Guild label with Dizzy's quintet in that period, became a demonstration record at the Juilliard School of Music in New York for ensemble playing lessons. Dizzy would reminisce on his seventieth birthday tribute on Columbia University's radio station, WKCR: "Yard and I were so close, so wrapped up in one another, that he would think 'three,' and I would say 'four,' and I would say 'seven,' and he'd say 'eight.' . . . It wasn't difficult for us, really together, sometimes it sounded like one horn playing, and sometimes it was one horn, but sometimes it was both of us sounding like one horn."

Miles Davis, then starting his career and never comfortable playing at fast tempos or in a very high register, marveled at the synchronization between Bird and Dizzy, and at how fast Bird could play. In part, Bird played so fast because the alto saxophone is easier to play fast than a trumpet, Miles knew. But Bird was still faster than anybody.

However, there was tragedy brewing in the relationship between Dizzy and Bird. Bird would be nearly asleep, nodding from heroin, and denying it to Dizzy, while Dizzy kept begging him to stop using drugs. Off the bandstand, Bird hung around with drug dealers and others in the drug culture. But Dizzy never actually saw Bird inject himself with drugs.

Dizzy and Bird never fought. But Dizzy became upset when Bird came late for performances. One night Bird arrived late and headed straight for the men's room, where, Dizzy knew, he was injecting himself with heroin. Disgusted, Dizzy blurted out on the bandstand to the other musicians that Bird was taking drugs at that very moment. Dizzy made his comment so near the microphone that the audience heard him. In the men's room, Bird heard the announcement, too. It could have attracted the police. He came out and complained to Dizzy. Max Roach recalled that later the men sat around, telling Bird how much he meant to his race and to the new music. They begged him to stop throwing his life away.

That's when Bird said he was getting famous through music for one reason: to call attention to the evils of drug addiction. He had been put on earth to scare people away from drugs. When his friends tried to save his life, he would say anything to justify his helplessness against the force of his habit.

Musicians also remembered the good times that Bird and Dizzy had together. They used to stage what was called an "ambush." With their horns under their coats, they would dash into a club on Fifty-second Street, jump up on a bandstand where other musicians were playing in a swing era style, and start playing, interrupting the music. But if the swing era players saw the beboppers first, the older fellows jumped off the bandstand, let the youngsters play for a few minutes, then got back on stage and mounted their own ambush. The audiences loved the action.

The good and bawdy times on Fifty-second Street healed Dizzy's wounds from the Hepsations tour. Then a call came in, inviting him to go to Los Angeles and play in Billy Berg's club. Berg had owned clubs since the 1930s, and he had even ended racial segregation in the audiences in the 1940s. Artistically and commercially, Berg was taking a chance by booking a group of beboppers for a Los Angeles audience. Nat King Cole's soft, easy sound appealed to Californians, so Berg didn't hire the beboppers as headliners. Dizzy, with his quintet, including Bird, was booked as the intermission entertainment. Bebop would get another test away from the hip Manhattan jazz lovers.

10

bebop comes of age

BILLY Berg specified that Bird had to be included in Dizzy's quintet. Dizzy was so leery of Bird's problems by then that he hired one of his favorite disciples, vibes player Milt Jackson, to go to California with the group. Dizzy wanted to be sure that five men were always on the bandstand. He didn't want the boss deducting money from the group's pay if Bird showed up late or missed performances. Dizzy delivered Bird's plane ticket and told him to be sure to get to the job. Bird promised, and he did get to California.

Just as Dizzy had thought, Bird didn't get to all the performances. When he did show up, the other musicians in the band thought the music played by Dizzy and Bird together was marvelous. Dizzy knew they had some "golden, magic, never fully appreciated moments" together on the bandstand. But the audience in California wanted to hear singers and wasn't interested in bebop. Dizzy tried to make the best of it and, to please the club owner, even sang a few words of "Salt Peanuts." But Dizzy kept looking forward to the day the gig was over.

Socializing all the time, Dizzy got to know and play with important musicians who lived on the West Coast. The men in his own band knew that Dizzy was friendly and protective of them, and he kept teaching them. Bird was using drugs of such a quality that they were making him sicker than ever. "He was out in the jungle somewhere, just lost, man," the drummer, Stan Levey, noted. Dizzy couldn't even find Bird to give him his plane ticket home. Dizzy and Lorraine left it, along with some money, at the hotel desk.

Bird didn't get back to New York until more than a year later, in 1947. He became so sick in California that he was taken to the Camarillo hospital and cured of his drug habits—for a while.

Leaving behind the bored audiences of Los Angeles, Dizzy was thrilled to find that he had become a star in New York. He was in demand in two clubs on Fifty-second Street, the Three Deuces and a bigger club, the Spotlite. Clark Monroe, who owned the Uptown House, where Dizzy had jammed many times, also owned the Spotlite. Monroe wanted Dizzy to come in first with a small group, then with a big band. Dizzy hired Sonny Stitt, an alto saxophonist, who had patterned himself after Bird.

Dizzy was still struggling financially. He even kept writing arrangements for other bands because he needed the money. But several more big boosts happened at that time. A musician Dizzy knew sent him to an excellent ear, nose, and throat doctor, Dr. Irving Goldman. Dizzy had a chronic lip infection. The doctor did some deep cleaning inside Dizzy's lip, and after that the infection and soreness went away. Dizzy was freer than ever to explore the horn. By that time, he was working with the brilliant young arranger Walter Gil Fuller. Fuller seemed to understand Dizzy's music perfectly, and he wrote challenging arrangements that used all of Dizzy's abilities.

When they worked together on Dizzy's songs, Gil supplied not only arrangements but also parts of the compositions at times. He helped Dizzy organize his new big band and rehearse the musicians. Dizzy leaned heavily on Gil's talents, and Gil depended on Dizzy, too, to play the arrangements so well and lead the band so magnificently that all the effort was worthwhile. Billy Eckstine was breaking up his band at that time. He gave the key to his office to Gil Fuller and told him to take anything he wanted—arrangements, microphones, even uniforms.

Gil and Dizzy were in love with the music, the men they hired, and the great publicity that Clark Monroe gave them for Dizzy Gillespie's big band opening at the Spotlite. They used music by Thelonious Monk and also by John Lewis, a classically trained pianist just home from the army. Drummer Kenny Clarke introduced John Lewis to Dizzy and Gil. They hired James Moody, a young saxophonist who was actually partially deaf. Moody was a brilliantly talented musician who overcame his handicap and became devoted to Dizzy.

The band kept playing wherever it found dates—in clubs, colleges, and theaters. When Charlie Parker came back to town, he joined it. For a while, he was healthy-looking, cured of drugs. But soon he was using heroin again. He showed up late for one performance, and it was obvious that he was almost asleep from the drugs. Dizzy was so upset he nearly threw Bird off the bandstand. Dizzy didn't want the younger musicians or the public to think that he approved of Bird in that condition. But Dizzy couldn't fire Bird himself. He asked someone else to do it.

Gil Fuller's arrangements featured all of Dizzy's strong talents, and the trumpeter stood out as a great star in that band. Many stars and future stars played for it. Ella Fitzgerald, who had hired Dizzy when he left Cab Calloway's band, now came to Dizzy for a job. He taught her how to scat sing. The technique, singing the nonsense vowel sounds that gave birth to the name "bebop" and heightened the excitement of the music, made Ella even more famous than she had been. She loved his song "Oo Bop Sha Bam a Klook a Mop," and she had great hits with scat sounds on "Lady Be Good" and "How High the Moon."

Dizzy made a film that year called *Jivin' in Bebop* which was a big success in the "colored theaters," and from time to time throughout his career he would appear in films.

On tour, Dizzy once stopped to do a show at the Laurinburg Institute, where he treated his old teacher, Alice Wilson, to tickets. She and most of the audience were puzzled by the music he was playing. Some people tried to dance.

Others just stood and gawked. But out of loyalty and pride in the man from Cheraw, they cheered Dizzy. After that, most people in Cheraw bought his records. Because of his growing successes on film and in performances, Dizzy was beginning to feel that he had "conquered" part of the world.

Lorraine helped him with financial management. She traveled with him and advised him—and cooked his eggs, too. Wherever he went, he always wanted Lorraine to cook his eggs. No one else would do. With Lorraine to manage, Dizzy was free to let his gifts and energy take him as far as he could go.

Where they took him at that time was on an adventure with Latin sounds—particularly Afro-Cuban music, the polyrhythmic music that had been developed by the drummers, the *conga*, *timbale*, and *quinto* players on the island of Cuba. There the musicians remained steeped in the drumming traditions of Africa. The blacks of Cuba had never been forbidden to play the drums, as African Americans had been when slavery existed in the United States.

Dizzy's big band was going strong in 1947 when he told his old friend, Mario Bauza, the Cuban who had helped him get a job in Cab Calloway's band, that he wanted to get a conga player for the band. Bauza knew just the man for Dizzy. A conga player named Chano Pozo had just arrived from Cuba. He was one of the most exciting players Bauza had ever heard. When Dizzy and Chano met, they couldn't speak a word to each other. Dizzy didn't speak Spanish, and Chano Pozo never learned English. Dizzy became fluent in imitating Chano's accent, and he would later write about how Chano explained their remarkable communication: "Deehee no peek pani, me no peek Angli, bo peek African." Chano meant that both of them could understand the language of the drums.

The Afro-Cuban rhythms were very different from the swing of jazz, but Dizzy found ways to blend Latin and jazz rhythms. First he and Chano wrote and played a song they called "Manteca," which means "lard." It became one of Dizzy's best-selling recordings. Dizzy and Chano developed "Manteca" with the help of Gil Fuller, who gave it structure. He arranged and orchestrated it. Then Dizzy, Chano, and a modern musician named George Russell wrote "Cubano Be, Cubano Bop." These exciting songs with an exotic flavor were among Dizzy's best-selling recordings.

Chano Pozo lacked discipline. His music needed the development and structure that Walter Gil Fuller could give it. Chano's life was mysterious and chaotic, too. Dizzy knew him as a "roughneck," even a "hoodlum," who traveled with a long knife. He was also a great musician who was, in Dizzy's words, "stone African"—completely African. That is, he was a master at playing the African spiritual rhythms that survived in Cuba.

There were several rumors about why Chano left Cuba. One tale said that he had gone to collect royalties from a man in Cuba. Instead of paying Chano, the man shot him. Chano went to New York with a bullet lodged dangerously close to his spine. Sometimes it gave him great pain when he played. Another rumor was that he had taken money that he should have left with his spiritual group in Cuba.

Dizzy's message of bebop spread with the exciting addition of Chano Pozo, a brilliant showman. The band went into Carnegie Hall for its first concert there on September 29, 1947, not only with Chano but with Charlie Parker. Dizzy was filled with pride when he read an advance story written by the critic Bill Gottlieb for a leading newspaper at the time, the *Herald Tribune*.

Gottlieb said that bebop was replacing swing: "Bebop is modern, progressive music, harmonically suited to the times. . . . Like other jazz forms before it, bebop, in diluted form, will eventually alter even the most commercial forms of popular music. It's begun to do so already. . . ." The concert was another great boost for Dizzy, Bird, and bebop. After one of the songs during the concert, Bird walked onstage and handed Dizzy a rose with a long stem. "He'd probably spent his last quarter to buy it," Dizzy thought. "And he kissed me on the mouth and then walked off. I get a warm feeling every time I think of Charlie Parker."

That year, too, *Metronome* magazine named Dizzy trumpeter of the year, and his band was the band of the year. Dizzy was rightfully proud of himself and reflected that his band was the best in the country at that time and deserved the award. Without mincing any words, he said he was competing with Count Basie, Duke Ellington, Woody Herman, Lionel Hampton, Tommy and Jimmy Dorsey, and Stan Kenton, the most famous of the big bands then. Dizzy didn't need a public relations expert. His steely nerve and resolve gave him the most help.

One of the country's most important jazz critics, Barry Ulanov, was boosting Dizzy, too. Ulanov was very enthusiastic about Dizzy's new recordings at that time, especially one of them, "Oop Pop a Da." Leonard Feather helped Dizzy by investing money in that first Carnegie Hall concert in 1947. At the time, Feather was a rising jazz writer, getting set to write and publish a small but important book, *Inside Bebop*. It was an exciting time for the smart young critics who liked the music.

Dizzy repeated his success with his band at Carnegie Hall in 1948, and he set off for a tour of Europe. He took Chano Pozo, drummer Kenny Clarke, and many other fine players, but the band traveled without Bird. He and Dizzy loved each other, but they never worked regularly together again because of Bird's addiction. For Dizzy, music was first. Inside Bird, music and drugs played a tug-of-war.

The tour of Europe was both the best and the worst of times for the band. First, the musicians endured a hurricane as they sailed to Sweden. The crew had to turn the ship around so that the waves wouldn't split it in half. Dizzy and his pianist, John Lewis, were among the few people aboard who didn't feel seasick or terrified. They went to all the meals and ate them for everybody else. The ship arrived in Sweden several days late, and the band had to hurry from the boat to a concert.

They played in many cities, and Swedish audiences loved their music. Dizzy, however, had an enormous problem with the Swedish tour promoter, Harold Lundquist. In plain words, Lundquist was a "crook," Dizzy said. Lundquist had agreed to deposit half of the band's money in a bank in the United States before the band ever left home. He didn't do it. He didn't pay the men after they arrived in Europe, either. The band's manager, Billy Shaw, whom Dizzy called by the nickname "Honey," flew to Europe to help Dizzy get the money. They had little success.

Dizzy slept outside the Swedish tour promoter's hotel door so that the man couldn't run off with the proceeds from the concerts. Milt Shaw, Billy's son, who was also traveling with the band was arrested for trying to kick Lundquist. Then Lundquist was arrested. The band got some of the money it had earned, and Billy Shaw managed to get a week's salary in advance from Lundquist for a trip to Belgium. The band went there to do concerts for the Hot Club of Brussels. In Europe, jazz fans had started forming social clubs where they listened to jazz recordings from America and sponsored performances by American musicians.

Dizzy ran out of money during the band's second week in Belgium. And then the Hot Club of Paris came to the band's rescue. The Paris club arranged for a big concert to take place at the Salle Pleyel, a concert hall in Paris. Parisian jazz fans were already excited by Dizzy's and Bird's recordings.

Dizzy's musicians arrived in Paris by train. They were exhausted and hungry (they had no money to buy food), and they may have been drinking, too, with their stomachs empty. The music they played was completely relaxed. If the band was not at its most polished because of the conditions under which it had been surviving, it was still a remarkably impressive group. The music they played heralded a new day for French audiences. Some important French critics fell in love with bebop. Others decided to hate it and never changed their minds. They became known as "the moldy figs." The Salle Pleyel concert was recorded in a primitive way on February 28, 1948, and became a jazz classic.

Dizzy would claim that the tour turned out to be a success commercially. He said the promoters were grossing fifteen thousand dollars on a good day with the band. But the band didn't get the approval of the Labor Department in England to tour there, because the British had a policy designed to protect British musicians from foreign competition. Tours of Italy and Spain were not arranged for Dizzy, either. It was the enthusiasm of the French that gave Dizzy such a good feeling.

11

new obstacles

THE American press remained divided about bebop for a while longer. *Time* magazine, which tended to be conservative, made fun of bebop. In a way *Time* was a moldy fig.

There were also prejudiced people who wanted to believe that white musicians had invented bebop. Some said Dizzy had copied bebop from Stan Kenton, a white bandleader who was playing a colder, less-swinging version of modern music. Kenton had started playing in his style only after he had studied Dizzy's music carefully. Kenton hired Latin conga players to help his imitation along, but he had done nothing special with the congas. He just let the musicians play whatever they felt like playing to add the excitement of their sound to a big band.

Bebop had its firm supporters, too. In Chicago, a radio disc jockey named Daddy-O Daylie, a favorite with musicians, decided to play bebop all the time because he realized that the African-American musicians needed all the support they could get.

Around every corner, Dizzy met with a new situation. In 1948 he had great success playing in Southern California. Though Bird was no longer playing with him, Dizzy performed some of Bird's music. "Relaxin' at Camarillo" was a recording Dizzy made at a Pasadena concert organized by a well-known jazz concert producer. Bebop was having success all over the country. Dizzy was such a great leader that he could encourage his musicians to play at the top of their powers. Once they even lost the sheet music when they were traveling, but Dizzy stayed calm and helped them to play the music by heart.

To his performances came celebrites. One of the most important was a screen actress named Ava Gardner, renowned as a great beauty. Wherever she went, she attracted attention. Another beautiful actress, Lena Horne, the most famous African-American woman of the time, and a fine actor named Howard Duff went to Dizzy's shows, too. Dizzy was a hot star.

There was also a flashy side to bebop. So some people treated the music as if it were a wild and nutty cult. In 1948 Dizzy started wearing horn-rimmed glasses, which called attention to his style. Then he began to wear dark glasses on stage to protect his eyes from the light. People thought he wore sunglasses onstage for effect, and fans started imitating him. Actually Dizzy wore sunglasses to cut down the glare of lights after his cataract surgery.

Dizzy also grew a goatee, because shaving every day irritated his bottom lip. He accidentally shaved off part of his mustache one day. Having done that, he shaved off the rest of it. This exposed the metal mark that a trumpet leaves on a trumpeter's lip after he has been playing for years. The mark on Dizzy looked like half a mustache. So people made fun of Dizzy for wearing half a mustache, not realizing they were looking at the trumpeter's proudly worn badge of profession.

Dizzy wore pegged pants and jackets with wide lapels. Then the beboppers took the lapels off and wore cashmere jackets with no lapels. That style became an elegant trendsetter, too, publicized in *Esquire* magazine. Dizzy also began wearing a beret at a time when men were still wearing fedoras with brims.

Beboppers were also criticized for using slang, some of it musicians' slang, some of it hip black English, most of it colorful, some of it obscene. It seems very tame compared to the slang used by rappers forty years later. Beboppers also came under fire for their freewheeling life-styles. African-American musicians were criticized for having love affairs with white women. It was true that African-American musicians were among the first to mingle socially with whites, both white men and women. Sometimes musicians did have love affairs with white women, and sometimes they married. More often, friendships began when white women who liked jazz asked their boyfriends or husbands to take them to jazz clubs. The men went along. If they liked the free, individualistic sound of the music, they lent their enthusiasm and support.

And rumors started that jazz musicians drank all the

time, used drugs, and went crazy with them. Playing in clubs all night, staying up until dawn, many musicians drank too much, and they had to learn to control themselves. In the 1940s some musicians started using heroin. Eventually, many stopped all their bad habits. They learned it was a lie that musicians had to drink and use drugs to play jazz. Most of them tried to live the healthiest lives they could, so that they could become excellent players and live a long time. The rumors about the wild lives of jazz musicians bothered Dizzy. He noticed that people mistook the rumors about musicians for the meaning of the music.

He also noticed that pop singers were beginning to put a few scat words in songs, and pop musicians were adding a few bebop phrases to their arrangements. They called the results bebop. But the tricks were just tricks, and the results were usually not very good pop. Pop musicians and their business backers made a great deal of money by loosely imitating the bebop style. Dizzy found his groups in competition with these more commercial-sounding group. If it hadn't been for Lorraine's frugal, sensible ways of handling money, he would have had nothing left over from all his travels, efforts, and fees.

In 1948, when Chano Pozo traveled south with the band on a tour, his drums were stolen. He returned to New York, where he was shot to death in the Rio Bar on 111th Street and Fifth Avenue. He and Dizzy had collaborated for only a year. Dizzy first heard that a drug dealer had shot Chano. Then Dizzy heard another rumor that he came to think might be true. Chano might have been killed for revenge on the first anniversary of the day he left Cuba with money belonging to his spiritual group. For Dizzy and his band, Chano's death was a terrible loss.

For the rest of his life, Dizzy enjoyed special friendships and communion with Latin musicians because they knew he loved their music. Latin rhythms would always play an important part in his life and career. He would eventually form an international big band—the United Nation Orchestra, he called it—that he had dreamed about for years, and it would contain a great number of Latin musicians. He helped sponsor the emigration of many Cuban musicians after relations between the United States and Communist Cuba became hostile. He hired them and helped them with their problems, just like a big brother, an uncle, or even a father.

Soon after Chano was killed, Dizzy led another concert at Carnegie Hall, where he performed a spiritual, "Nobody Knows the Trouble I've Seen," as a tribute to the Cuban drummer.

Despite the honors he won for playing at Carnegie Hall and for inspiring musicians to play modern music and dream of extensions of bebop, and despite all the fans he won over who went to his performances and bought his recordings, Dizzy was about to suffer from a sudden downturn in his fortunes. People had been fascinated for a while by the new music. But they wanted a simple beat for dancing and romancing.

Teenagers didn't want to take the time to learn to appreciate bebop, a high-style, sophisticated music. Soldiers home from World War II wanted easy, slow music to relax with. The soldiers going off to war again in Korea wanted simple love songs and melodies to keep in their minds. Fans stopped swarming to hear bebop. All the beboppers were facing hard times. Because Dizzy wasn't earning enough money, he had to let his band go. He went to work at a club called Snookie's in the New York City borough of Queens. After a while he was able to work at Birdland, a new club around the corner from Fifty-second Street. He played in front of a rhythm section—a piano, bass, and drum trio. Birdland was making a name for itself as the greatest jazz club that had ever existed. Sometimes Bird played there, too with a string section. Even though Birdland had been named for Bird, he never led his own group there in those years.

Dizzy occasionally played with the group Bird was working with, and Bird was a guest in Dizzy's group. But they weren't hired to work together. To make ends meet financially, Dizzy actually worked as a soloist and traveled with Stan Kenton's band. Kenton could find jobs. Dizzy didn't lose heart, though. Years later he would remember about his solos in front of the Kenton band: "It was beautiful, you know, because there was such a great deal of respect from the musicians in the band. These guys had their mouths open all night, man. It was dynamite!"

Bird, too, toured with Kenton, and as usual he spent too much time half-asleep on the bandstand. This time it was because he was trying to stop using heroin by substituting a fifth of whiskey a day. Dizzy scolded him one night, telling him how one of Kenton's fine white alto saxophone players was making Bird look like a fool. Bird snapped to attention, stopped drinking, and played soulfully.

Dizzy ran a colorful campaign for president of the United States in 1964. (Charles Fishman)

Dizzy leading his group; Mike Longo, piano; Paul West, bass; Candy Finch, drums; and James Woods, tenor sax (Institute of Jazz Studies, Rutgers University)

Dizzy Gillespie, 1973 (Raymond Ross Photography)

Dizzy on *Sesame Street*, 1982 (A&S Shevette/Children's Television Workshop; reprinted by permission of the estate of Dizzy Gillespie)

May 19, 1987: Dizzy receives an honorary degree from the New School for Social Research (Raymond Ross Photography)

Dizzy with his protégé, trumpeter Jon Faddis (Bill May, Omnivision)

Dizzy, at the White House with President George Bush, meets the president of Senegal. (Charles Fishman)

Dizzy warms up backstage with his friend Dave Usher at the Montreux Jazz Festival in Detroit, Michigan, in 1990. (Dave Usher)

Dizzy becomes Bashere of Iperu in Lagos, Nigeria, January 1990. (Dave Usher)

Dizzy

(© Telarc International; Frank Micelotta)

Trying to find a way to keep playing his own fiery music, Dizzy decided to form his own small group with six musicians. He also started his own recording company, DeeGee Records, with the help of a friend, Dave Usher. The friendship far outlived the company, which soon fell far behind in its payment of taxes. The taxes were paid eventually, and Dizzy was very proud of some of the recordings he made with DeeGee. But after the recordings were leased to another company, the business became troubled again, and it didn't recover.

Dizzy knew he had failed with DeeGee Records because of inexperience. Then, by chance, he made a recording that could have brought him riches. It was a tape of a concert billed as "The Greatest Jazz Concert Ever," held at Massey Hall in Toronto, Canada. It starred Dizzy, drummer Max Roach, Bird, pianist Bud Powell, and the bassist and bold composer, Charles Mingus. Mingus, an unusual character and an experimental musician, decided to tape the concert, because he was starting his own recording company. Dizzy was very happy with the music that the group played that night. He thought that Bird sounded wonderful. Even though Bird was in delicate condition physically, "that night he was ready to play," Dizzy would recall.

After the concert, each man put his check in his pocket and went away. Dizzy went home and put the check on the dresser. He thought that Lorraine would take care of the money as usual. Bird took his check to the ticket booth at the concert hall and got it cashed. He needed his money right away to support his habit. When Lorraine put Dizzy's check in the bank later, it bounced. Max, Bud, and Mingus had the same experience. Dizzy was never able to get paid for the concert. He saw the man in charge of concert finances many times throughout the following years. The man always smiled and said hello, but he never did anything about the bad check.

Then came the news that Charles Mingus had gone through a divorce. As part of the settlement, he gave his wife his new recording company. The tape of the concert at Massey Hall went to her. Mingus never received a penny from sales of the recording, and neither did Dizzy or anyone else who played in the concert.

It was no wonder that Dizzy would eventually say he didn't like to look back. He only liked to think about the present or the future. He had learned to protect his spirit and survive by never concentrating on all the wildly difficult times he had lived through. For courage and happiness, he kept turning to his trumpet.

Something new was added to his trumpet in 1953. The comedy team Stump and Stumpy were fooling around at a party, and one of them fell on Dizzy's horn. The bell was bent so that it stuck up at a funny angle, pointing toward the ceiling. Instead of getting upset, Dizzy tried to play the instrument that way. He liked the sound. People thought he might be able to hear himself better. Most of all, the unique shape of the horn became a conversation piece. It added to Dizzy's image as a character and a showman.

Even though the check for the Massey Hall concert bounced, Dizzy and Lorraine were not impoverished. They were living in Corona, Queens, just outside of Manhattan, in a house that Dizzy bought with the help of a loan from one of the owners of Birdland, Morris Levy. Levy withheld some of Dizzy's salary each time Dizzy played at Birdland, to pay back the loan, and never charged interest. Levy made a lot of money in Birdland and one day he showed his gratitude to Dizzy by handing him a box full of cash. It was the money that Levy had withheld as the loan repayment. He was giving it back.

A young man named George Wein, who owned Storyville, then the leading jazz club in Boston, had hired Dizzy to play there. When George founded the Newport Jazz Festival in Rhode Island in 1954, he booked Dizzy for the opening. Dizzy's constant efforts and excellence always saved the day for him. Someone always wanted him to play. He never complained, because music was his life. Though the rest of the world could hold all the unexpected surprises and conflicting passions of a jungle, he knew he could control his music.

12

milestones

IN June 1953, a month after the concert in Toronto, Dizzy and Bird played together for a broadcast. Bird joined Dizzy's regular quintet for that performance only. Then they went their separate ways and never recorded together again. Bird was becoming sicker. He was so unreliable that he was finding it difficult to get jobs.

Dizzy was working at Birdland in 1955. During an intermission, he decided to take a walk to a famous basement club called Basin Street East on Fifty-second Street. Trumpeter Charlie Shavers, Dizzy's old friend, was playing there in clarinetist Benny Goodman's group. By chance, Bird happened to be in the audience, and he and Dizzy started talking. In his book, *To BE or Not . . . to BOP*, Dizzy wrote:

> He walked up to me and said, "Diz, why don't you save me?"
>
> And I saw the expression on his face. It was a pained expression . . . and I didn't know what to say. I said, "What could I do?"
>
> He said, "I dunno but just save me, save me, man."
>
> I didn't know what to do. I just didn't know what to say to that man. I didn't know what to say because I already had my group, and he was just jobbing around. He wasn't doing too well. Maybe I shoulda. That woulda been the moment to get back together, I think, but I already had my group and we were on this level, and I didn't think anything of it too much, because he'd been doing his thing. Right after that, he died. We never played together again. It hit me pretty hard . . . but I don't feel that I let him down in any way, not necessarily. When a dude is using drugs, no one can help him. You have to have that determination to pull yourself up. Because regardless of how much someone does try to help you, if you've got in your mind to keep using, it doesn't matter. Drug addicts don't have any sense of, well, there's a guy helping me, maybe I ought to straighten up. They gotta wanna straighten up themselves. And they do it alone.

Dizzy also knew that if he took Bird into the group, Bird might not even show up. "What came to my mind was if we could get back together, we'd go someplace and have a contract for five guys, and there'd be only four of us there, just like when I took him to California and paid for six guys instead of five. . . . It seemed logical to me to have someone who played a little less and was there all the time than to have this super-super-duper guy who sometimes wouldn't be there, and you'd have to go through a bunch of changes. So I didn't want to."

Bird died on March 12, 1955, in the luxurious apartment of a patroness of jazz. Musicians around the country mourned. Dizzy went down to the basement of his house in Queens and "cried like a baby for a week," Lorraine reported. After his death graffiti scrawls began appearing around the country, proclaiming "Bird Lives!" But Bird had never become a commercial superstar during his lifetime. He had left no money to his wives or children, only debts. There wasn't even any money to bury him.

Dizzy contacted Norman Granz, founder of a group called Jazz at the Philharmonic, which sponsored touring jazz concerts. Both Dizzy and Bird had worked for Granz. Granz paid the cost of shipping Bird's body to his mother for burial in Kansas City. Dizzy and a group of musicians who had loved Bird's music started a committee to try to organize Bird's musical legacy. Lorraine was worried about how strongly Dizzy reacted to Bird's early death. She convinced him to stop working on the committee to save Bird's music and to keep his mind on his own work.

Dizzy was obliged to keep working hard in those lean times for bebop. On a weekend, he would dash out of town to play in Philadelphia, then come back to New York to play more. Other musicians gave the Bird project time, but in the end, Bird's music lived on because everyone listened to it. Musicians played it. Dizzy went all over the world playing "our music," as he called it. He tried to make sure that Bird got full credit.

By the summer of 1955, Dizzy began teaching jazz at the Lenox School of Jazz in Lenox, Massachusetts. It was located in a lovely green and hilly part of the country, where Dizzy felt refreshed and comforted. He was tired of running from club to club. He had the company of other jazz musicians, and also the Boston Symphony Orchestra, which played in the summer at Tanglewood in Lenox. The atmosphere inspired him to write a song called "Wheatleigh Hall." It wasn't his most exciting song, but it was a tribute to the place he stayed that summer. Corporations and music industry companies funded the jazz school. Dizzy was happy that society was beginning to recognize jazz as a great American art form. "Yard would have enjoyed it had he lived," Dizzy wrote in his book.

Progress in giving jazz musicians the credit they deserved was slow, but it was under way. Jazz at the Philharmonic required that all audiences for its concerts be integrated. The television networks were hiring African-Americans as well as whites to work as studio musicians. And because of the influence of a great African-American congressman, Adam Clayton Powell, Dizzy received a special honor. He was chosen as the first jazzman to represent the U.S. State Department for a cultural mission—a tour of the Near East, the Middle East, and Asia.

He was on his way out the door of his house in 1956, going to play in a Jazz at the Philharmonic concert in Europe, when he was called about the cultural mission. He left the business details for Lorraine to handle. Dizzy was "highly honored," he said, and he was also delighted that the State Department was going to pay for all costs.

In his band he had "blacks, whites, females, Jews, and Gentiles," he wrote. One female was a vocalist—that was usual. But wonder of wonders, Dizzy also hired a female trombonist named Melba Liston. In those days women never played any kind of horn in the big bands. Dizzy chose Melba not only because she was such a wonderful player, but because she was an even greater arranger. Dizzy wanted the luxury of traveling with his arranger. At first the men in his band insulted her. Then they heard her play and saw the music she wrote for them, and they started saying, "Mama's all right." Melba later wrote: "Dizzy was greatly responsible for the love and respect that I got. . . . He wouldn't let anyone abuse me too much in the band. . . ."

Some musicians wanted to try to play better than Dizzy. That was all the motivation he needed to catch fire every night. Nobody outshone him. The band gave its first performance in Iran and went on to Lebanon, which had an American University at that time. Dizzy was astounded at the breathtaking beauty of Beirut, Lebanon, which he called "God's earth." There he played two concerts for 1,500 people; then he had to arrange for a third performance. The band flew to Pakistan, where Dizzy found out that tickets cost five dollars each. The poor people couldn't afford them, so he took 150 from the impresario for a concert and gave them away.

His zest for living and his fearlessness led him into great

adventures. He joined a snake charmer's act and played trumpet. His trumpet went too close to a cobra's head. The cobra was supposed to be defanged, but when it hissed, Dizzy moved away fast. "I set a world record backward broad jump," he joked, recalling; "I must have jumped back fifteen feet." None of the other American musicians went near the snake and its basket.

He loved the native musicians and their unfamiliar instruments in Pakistan, and he learned some Eastern music scales; he later made recordings using the exotic scales as the basis for his melodies. He was invited to a late-night party in Pakistan. A ricksha driver was assigned to take him there. Lorraine was worried about Dizzy going off with the driver into the pitch-black night, but Dizzy had no fear. He talked the ricksha driver into letting him drive the bicycle. On the way, Dizzy started playing his horn, too. A flute player standing on a roof along the route joined in. Dizzy loved the beauty of the moment, when he played in harmony with an unseen stranger. At the party, Dizzy tried to play with the Pakistani musicians.

One day he spotted a little boy about twelve years old in the alleyway to the stage entrance. The boy was wearing ragged clothes, and he had no shoes. Dizzy took the child to buy a long shirt and some shoes, much to the horror of the Pakistanis who were taking care of the tour. They worried that the boy would rob Dizzy. Then they were upset that Dizzy put the child on his lap in the car to take him to a clothing store. When Dizzy bought the boy shoes, the Pakistanis said the child would sell his shoes right away, because none of his friends wore shoes. Dizzy didn't care if the little boy sold his shoes to get food. Dizzy could remember the days when he didn't have shoes to wear to church for Easter. He didn't tell the Pakistanis about his own memories of poverty.

When people asked Dizzy about racism in the United States, he said: "We have our problems, but we're still working on it. I'm the leader of the band, and those white guys are working for me. That's a helluva thing. A hundred years ago, our ancestors were slaves, and today we're scuffling with this problem, but I'm sure it's gonna be straightened out some day. I probably won't see it, completely, the eradication of racial prejudice in the United States, but it will be eliminated." That is what he said that day, and he put it in his book. He would not always feel so hopeful. In private he sometimes said that he did not think the problem would ever go away. He always felt more comfortable with his own people, he would reflect.

Turkey, Syria, and Greece were also on the list of countries for the tour. Again in Turkey he insisted that the poor people, who were being kept out of the concerts, be allowed in to hear his band. In Greece he arrived at a time when students were throwing rocks at the United States Information Service office in Athens. But during the concert, Dizzy heard "Bravo, Bravo!" from the students. The newspaper headlines said, "Greek Students Lay Down Rocks and Roll with Diz."

Dizzy even played a superb concert at seven in the morning in Athens. When a USIS official wanted him to bring all the musicians to play another set at a cocktail party after a concert, Dizzy refused. The official was angry, but Dizzy was even more annoyed, because the official, who had been drinking too much, had no right to ask for an extra performance. Dizzy made a report of the incident. The State Department was very happy with the way Dizzy conducted the tour and the great success jazz had abroad. Dizzy knew exactly how to lead. He was a rarity in the world, not only a born musician and a revolutionary, but an ideal leader to carry on after the revolution had become a fact. The tour revived his career after the fad of bebop had passed. He was a brighter star than he had ever been before.

When he came home, he met President Dwight D. Eisenhower, and the tour band made a recording. Soon afterward he was sent to lead the band on a tour of Latin America. He was already in love with Afro-Cuban music. Now he heard the soft, exciting samba rhythms of Brazil, which seemed as subtle and natural as breathing. Dizzy learned even more about Latin rhythms, and he found out there were many "brothers" in Brazil. He felt the common bond of their African musical heritage. The exotic Brazilian rhythm instruments—the *berimbau*, made from a gourd, for example—charmed him. And he was happy to see that some "brothers" in Brazil had positions of importance. One was a chief arranger at a television studio.

Dizzy heard about the province of Bahia in Brazil, where so many black people lived, and the home of most of the creative music of Brazil. He didn't have time to go there, but many Bahians came to his hotel and serenaded him. They knew who he was. He put Bahia on his private list of places he wanted to go to one day. The music in Brazil taught him about the "oneness of music," because he heard Brazilian musicians playing music that sounded to him just like lines that he and Charlie Parker had played. The Brazilians put their own samba rhythm behind the music, which came from the same African heritage.

In Argentina, which Dizzy loved because it had so much Spanish influence, he met important musicians. Some would eventually go to the United States and become stars. Dizzy inspired them and even commissioned one of them, Lalo Schifrin, a pianist, to write music for him. Dizzy eventually hired him to play in his group, too.

When he returned to North America, he led the band, which was filled with young jazz stars, in a very successful concert for prisoners on Rikers Island in New York City. For a while he toured by himself with Jazz at the Philharmonic. He could always make a good fee from JATP. And the next year he reorganized the tour's big band and traveled with it from Canada down to Atlanta, Georgia, where he played for an integrated audience. "Whites were still struggling to hold onto segregation" in Georgia, he knew. Since he had been sent around the world with an integrated big band to make a good impression on foreign countries, he thought it was the right time to bring the message home to Americans. Nothing seemed to be too difficult for him to attempt, on or off the bandstand.

In the Atlanta airport he was asked to wait until some white people took care of their tickets before he was served. He refused, and the police were called into the argument. Dizzy stood up to the threat, while the rest of the band watched in fright.

The cost of the trips abroad annoyed some congressmen. Dizzy told them that American jazz was obviously far more appreciated abroad than in the United States. The State Department defended the cost of the tours, saying that the United States couldn't afford to send less than the very best artists abroad.

There was no doubt that Dizzy was regarded as among the best everyplace. He played for an integrated audience in his hometown, which declared a Dizzy Gillespie Day in 1959. He went to visit an old white man named Powe in Cheraw. Dizzy's mother's last name was Powe, and Dizzy remembered that his mother had worked in the Powes's kitchen. Mr. Powe, who was sick, was delighted to see Dizzy, and invited him to sit down in the living room. Dizzy had never seen that family's living room until then. Mr. Powe told Dizzy about how Dizzy's great-grandmother had been the daughter of an African chief. Dizzy said that Mr. Powe should therefore call him "your majesty." That made Mr. Powe laugh with hilarity. Then Mr. Powe told Dizzy more about his great-grandmother and Dizzy was able to figure out that Mr. Powe's grandfather was Dizzy's great-grandfather. Now it was Dizzy's turn to laugh heartily.

13

dizzy stays on the road

IN 1959 Dizzy's mother died. Dizzy reckoned she was seventy-four at the time. She had been sick and losing weight for some time. He felt she had waited for him to come home from a tour to say good-bye. It was the third time Lorraine saw Dizzy unbearably upset. Once was when he had to have an operation for cataracts on his eyes; Bird's death was another major blow. And now Dizzy cried for his mother. After she died, he began to think of ways he could contribute to the good of mankind.

He would sometimes think about starting a jazz school in France. He bought land in France with that goal in mind, but Lorraine had no desire to move to France. The

Gillespies bought a house in Englewood, New Jersey, which Lorraine decorated and landscaped. And Dizzy's life continued as a round of performances all over the world and homecomings to Lorraine.

At home and abroad he always liked going out to dinner with friends. People were always inviting him to be their guest. If he took a walk down the street, he spent a long time going only a few blocks. He knew everybody, and everybody knew him. He stopped to talk with the famous and the little people.

Throughout the 1960s he kept building his reputation. Rock music had become popular, and Dizzy worked constantly to keep jazz in the public eye and ear. He was a guest on the most important variety and talk shows on television. He made several movies, including one short, animated film called "The Hole." It featured an African-American man and a white man talking about greed as the reason for war. The film won an Academy Award. And he kept playing in clubs, concerts, and festivals. In every year, from 1947 to the end of his life, he was awarded one of the highest ratings for trumpeters in the jazz magazine polls. Sometimes he was in first place, sometimes second, always near the top. In 1960 he went into the *Down Beat* magazine Hall of Fame for jazz musicians.

Because of his wide-ranging interests, his understanding of public events, and his forceful personality, he decided to run for president of the United States in 1964. He had many supporters in the music world. They wanted to make a statement against the candidacy of the ultraconservative Republican candidate, Barry Goldwater. The campaign was full of humor. But underlying it was Dizzy's serious mission to try to help eliminate racism in music and every other area of the United States. He said he would change the name of the White House to the Blues House. To a *Down Beat* magazine writer, Dizzy said the key issues in the country were to establish civil rights, to remove or reduce the income tax through a national lottery, to give diplomatic recognition to China, to end the war in Vietnam, to give more federal support and money to the arts, and to promote equal opportunity in employment for people of all races.

President Lyndon Johnson won the election. Dizzy didn't get on the ballot in any state, though he did receive some write-in votes. But several of Dizzy's campaign goals became the law of the land during the Johnson administration and in the few years following. Johnson named Thurgood Marshall as the first African American to the U.S. Supreme Court. Equal opportunity laws went into effect. By 1968 colleges and music schools began taking jazz musicians onto their faculties. Minority group teenagers were given scholarships to study for degrees in jazz. And the National Endowment for the Arts finally recognized jazz as an art form and began giving grants to jazz musicians.

Dizzy watched as many of the musicians he had helped in their careers became stars. Miles Davis, a trumpeter, became a major rival for the position of the most popular trumpeter in the world. Miles played a cool style of jazz, an extension of bebop. He played far fewer notes than Dizzy, wasn't a high note player, and didn't rely upon the chords for inspiration for his melodies and harmonies. Most different was his tone, haunting and eerie. Dizzy's remained fiery, excited, and joyous. Pianist John Lewis became one of the founders of the Modern Jazz Quartet. The group emphasized European musical values for another extension of bebop—this one very disciplined and controlled. There were many other impressive, innovative musicians trying to put their own styles and ideas before the public. Dizzy had helped most of them.

A few musicians left the rhythmic and harmonic traditions of bebop so far behind that they were playing atonal music. They sounded a bit like the modern European classical composers. Most audiences didn't like the music. They certainly couldn't dance to it. They usually couldn't make sense out of it. It didn't have any melody. Jazz clubs started to lose customers. Those musicians ended up playing in their apartments for one another, earning no money. Nobody would pay to hear them.

A simpler form of music, called rhythm and blues when played by African Americans, and called rock and roll when played by whites, became so popular that traditional jazz musicians found it difficult to get any jobs at all. The new popular music used few chords, but the songs were catchy. Young people could sing along and dance.

Rock concerts with thousands of people in the audiences became the entertainment for the masses. Soon many people were protesting the war in Vietnam, smoking marijuana, and using drugs—and going to rock concerts. Jazz musicians had mainly quit using drugs, but teenage rock fans were getting in trouble with them. Rock music became so loud that people couldn't talk or think while they listened.

Rock concerts became dangerous, because fights broke out. Teenagers started to stay away from them. And a strange thing happened to jazz. It became popular again.

Dizzy's life didn't really change. He kept recording, appearing on television and in films, and traveling to play in all kinds of clubs and concerts. Though rock groups had replaced many jazz musicians in the limelight, Dizzy remained a star. Sophisticated audiences always came to hear him. He continued to receive awards and tributes. In the 1970s, as jazz again became popular, they started to come in faster.

Some of the older musicians were not able to find jobs playing music anymore. By this time it was plain to Dizzy that the music scene had changed totally. Big bands broke up after World War II, when it became too expensive to move them around the country. To survive, musicians had to know how to read music well, so they could qualify for jobs in the recording studios. Dizzy noticed that some of the musicians who had been unfair to him in Teddy Hill's band couldn't get studio jobs.

In the 1970s, when he was getting ready to go to Europe as a star and a bandleader, as he had done countless times by then, he reflected, "I'm at the top of my profession and playing better every day. All the musicians respect me, and I respect them. I respect talent. The older musicians are the guardians of the music, but that's not an excuse to keep people down and try to destroy their talent."

And he had grown older and wiser. He had almost stopped drinking alcohol, because he saw how much trouble it could get him into. In the earlier days he had been in some fights and later couldn't always remember how they had started. That didn't happen to him anymore. Through friends who brought him reading material, he had found a religion that gave him the spiritual support that he was hungry for, he said. He wanted to believe in the "oneness of mankind," he would come to say. That idea was the guiding principle of the Baha'i religion. The Baha'is taught unity. "I latched onto that," Dizzy would explain. And the Baha'i religion, which had started in the nineteenth century, had never had any connection to slavery or racial prejudice.

During the time when rock was so popular, Louis Armstrong and Duke Ellington had died. Dizzy was one of the best-known remaining jazz superstars. In the early 1970s, he started to get nominations from the National Association of Recording Arts and Sciences for the best jazz recordings. In 1975 he won his first Grammy for a recording with one of the best jazz pianists, Oscar Peterson.

To Dizzy went honorary degrees from colleges, keys to many cities in the country, and honors from jazz groups of all kinds. Dizzy was especially proud of the Paul Robeson Award he received from Rutgers University's Institute of Jazz Studies in 1972. To Dizzy, Robeson was a hero. Robeson had been denounced as a Communist, and he had lost out on many career opportunities because the State Department had denied him a passport. Dizzy revered Robeson—an African-American hero—as a great sports figure, a lawyer, an actor, and one of the greatest bass singers the country has ever known.

Dizzy had earned a lot of money, which Lorraine had

taken care of very well. They owned their house without owing a penny to anyone, he said. He drove an old, well-kept Mercedes-Benz with a sunroof. (Lorraine did not like him to drive it outside the neighborhood, because he drove too fast and had been involved in a few serious accidents. He usually had a chauffeur to drive.) In a mellower frame of mind than he had ever been in before, Dizzy was ready to become acknowledged as the leader of jazz musicians. Still a tireless player and constant traveler, he was ready to reap whatever reward the world had to offer.

Some people said Dizzy didn't always play with as much freshness, fire, and brilliance as he had possessed in the 1940s. But only the most gifted musician or critic could ever detect any change for the worse in Dizzy's work. After so many years of playing he usually sounded more mature and polished. His enthusiasm for jazz and for good young players helped keep him excited about his work. Sometimes he played something new and surprising. That kept him enthusiastic, too.

A trumpeter named Jon Faddis became Dizzy's protégé. Jon would eventually tell the press that he had been fifteen years old when he went backstage to meet Dizzy and ask him to sign his collection of Dizzy's work—fifty albums!

Dizzy listened to Jon play trumpet and began teaching him; then he started recording with Jon and taking him along to all sorts of jobs. Jon is one of the strongest, most passionate, and most proficient high-note players in the history of jazz trumpet. Dizzy not only taught Jon technique, but passed on to him, too, the sound of the joy of living.

Dizzy and Lorraine had no children of their own. Returning from one trip to Europe, Dizzy brought home a little dog. It was so tiny that Dizzy was able to carry it into the house in the turned-up cuff of his new suede coat with a sheepskin lining. He named it Maestro. Lorraine quickly trained it so that it knew which rooms were off-limits. Dizzy marveled at how thoroughly Lorraine could train even a little dog.

Lorraine developed a special affection for one of Dizzy's young relatives, and took him to live with them. It was always obvious to Dizzy's friends that he had a way with children. They loved him, and he loved them. Once, he dressed up in a swami's costume and went on the children's television show *Sesame Street*. Sitting cross-legged on the floor, wiggling his head from side to side, he sang "Swing Low, Sweet Cadillac," his spoof of the spiritual "Swing Low, Sweet Chariot." Friends thought it was too bad that he and Lorraine never had any children of their own.

Lorraine was glad that as he got older, Dizzy calmed down. He had diabetes, and it upset Lorraine that he didn't eat the right foods. He tried to control himself, but the truth was—he was in love with food, good rich food. Everywhere he went, he was treated to the best meals. He couldn't resist them.

But Dizzy was physically strong. Even as he approached seventy, he was able to work as if he were thirty years old. He told a newspaper reporter that he wanted to retire to his land in France and start a school one day, but he showed no signs of settling down. In the early 1980s, the new jazz clubs that were thriving in Greenwich Village in New York clubs that were thriving in Greenwich Village in New York City produced a jazz festival. To start it off, they staged a concert in a park and asked Dizzy Gillespie to star. Thousands of people showed up to hear him play. Some climbed trees to get a better view. That kind of adulation made Dizzy very happy. Later in the 1980s he started talking about his advancing years. "I'm almost seventy years old," he told everyone. But it was hard for people to take him seriously. He never said he was too tired.

14

some dreams are fulfilled

IN 1987 Dizzy made his sixth trip to Brazil to lead his band in the big, busy commercial city of São Paulo. The promoters of the tour had arranged a trip to Bahia for him, fulfilling his thirty-year dream. As soon as he finished performing, he packed a little overnight bag and got ready to go to Salvador, the main city in the province of Bahia, where African slaves had once landed in Brazil, and which was still mainly black.

His friend Dave Usher went with him. It didn't matter that DeeGee Records had failed. Their friendship was solid, as so many of Dizzy's friendships with lawyers, businessmen, and musicians were. People might go through terrible disappointments, but their love for one another survived.

When Dizzy got to Salvador on a Sunday, a Brazilian musician named Geronimo and his girlfriend took Dave and Dizzy to see the beach. He and Dave joined a crowd of people dancing on the shore. Dizzy felt happy in Bahia. He always felt at home in places like Jamaica, Kenya, Bahia—places where it was obvious that black people were in the majority. He was sick of racial prejudice. He liked being anyplace where he could have a rest from that problem. Even though race relations had changed a great deal in the United States, he would say that he still never felt as comfortable with whites as he did with black people.

It was not that he was narrow-minded. For a long time by then, Dizzy had considered himself a citizen of the world. He commanded respect as a public figure, and he demonstrated a deep commitment to peaceful relations with people of all races. "The earth is but one country, and mankind its citizen," he stated.

In Salvador he found out that Geronimo was going to perform that night. Dizzy listened to Geronimo for an hour and then went to sleep in his hotel room.

Awaking at eight in the morning, Dizzy found another Brazilian musician waiting to take him and Dave to Rio de Janeiro. This musician had once made an album and had asked Dizzy to play only one note on it. Dizzy had thought that was "real cute," he said. So he played accompaniment for a whole song. Then the fledgling musician was able to put Dizzy's name on the record cover and promote sales. Dizzy was glad to do it. He thought musicians were the least prejudiced people in the world. He loved them, and he loved music. No matter how much contribution a man made to music, there was always more to be done and learned.

The plane trip home from Rio took nine hours and got Dizzy to New York at 6:30 A.M. on a Tuesday. A limousine was waiting for him. The car had been sent by the New School for Social Research in New York City, which was getting ready to give him an honorary doctorate degree. Dizzy went directly to the school's ceremony at the First Presbyterian Church, a lovely old church on lower Fifth Avenue.

He put on a black cap and gown, which covered his traveling clothes—flashy black-and-white slacks and an even more eye-catching T-shirt with a picture of Kermit the Frog across the front. He sat down in the church with several other people who were also being given honorary degrees on that overcast, drizzly day.

Dizzy had lost count of the honorary degrees he had received by then. He thought he had a dozen. In the years to come, he would collect a total of nineteen. So far they had come from famous schools such as Tufts University in Boston, Fairleigh Dickinson University near his home in New Jersey, and the University of South Carolina, where he had not been allowed to set foot as a young man. Some of his music scores were in the archives at Clark University, but that school hadn't acknowledged him with a degree. It annoyed him that he had not yet received a doctorate from a black college. He wanted that sort of tribute to jazz—and to himself—from a black school.

He also thought it would be nice if he got doctorates from the Sorbonne in Paris and Oxford in England. In

France in 1989 he would receive an arts and letters award from the French government—as *Commandant d'ordre des arts et lettres*. Columbia University would number among the Ivy League schools that gave him doctorates. In wishing for some of these awards, he showed that he had lost none of his youthful confidence, boldness, and ambitious spirit. When asked how old he felt, he told someone he felt "all ages."

He was not conceited. Though he was really happy to have the new degree from the New School, he didn't brag about it. Afterward he would tell people about the fun of meeting interesting people at the ceremony. He sat next to a German woman, a West German editor and writer, an activist against fascism. She received a doctor of humane letters degree. When his name was called for him to accept his degree, it came with a message:

> Pioneering composer, legendary performer, musical genius. You charted new territory in jazz, expanding the musical vocabulary of our time. You created music of dazzling rhythmic complexity and enriched it with harmonic colors never heard before. You led a revolution in jazz. . . . Directly you have shaped the careers of many young musicians. . . . You have inspired others to challenge the limits of the herd. . . . You stand as a giant in the musical world, a force in winning recognition for jazz as a pillar of American culture and creativity. . . .

After the ceremony, Dizzy made the rounds of receptions—one in a nearby school library, another at the home of the president of the New School, and then a luncheon. Everywhere Dizzy went, people noticed his T-shirt, a sign that his brash, inventive spirit remained alive, well, and unselfconscious in the midst of solemn honors.

Halfway through the luncheon, Dizzy decided to steal a few quiet hours for himself at home. He was due to go in the evening to radio station WKCR at Columbia University, at the other end of Manhattan.

For seven days, twenty-four hours a day, Phil Schaap, a jazz historian and the station's curator and jazz authority, had been playing nearly every record that Dizzy had ever made. The reason was the fiftieth anniversary of Dizzy's first recording date with Teddy Hill. Later that same year, Dizzy would turn seventy years old.

At 5:00 P.M. it was time for Dizzy to set out with Bob Redcross, his chauffeur, to drive back to New York. At the radio station, Phil Schaap was begging phone callers to stay away. An audience couldn't fit into the tiny studio. The festival on radio was equal to a course in jazz history. Few men had played or recorded as much as Dizzy. Schaap asked Dizzy about tiny details of his career. Dizzy answered questions about things that had happened forty years earlier. It was astounding how much he could remember.

Normally Dizzy didn't think about the past, unless it was to remind himself not to repeat something. But Phil Schaap's questions and the records he was playing charmed Dizzy so much that he decided to stay on the air for three hours. Schaap had recordings that Dizzy had never heard, even though he had made them.

Dizzy was surprised to find out how many records he

had made. "I must have started recording in 1912," he joked. He said he had been given doctorates because he had been around so long. The cadences of the South were still in his speech. But the sophistications of years spent traveling, performing, and meeting people in all walks of life and in every possible circumstance made themselves evident, too. Then he began to yawn a lot. He said that he had been awake for twenty-four hours. Actually, except for a few naps, he had not slept for over a day and a half. So he said good night to Phil and to saxophonist Jimmy Heath, who showed up for the broadcast. Dizzy and Jimmy had been friends for decades. And Bob Redcross drove Dizzy back to Englewood.

The day—or rather, the series of days strung together—had been a typical chain of events in Dizzy's life on the road. Closer to his birthday that year, at Wolf Trap, in Virginia, there was a seventieth birthday tribute to him. The Wolf Trap festival sent a train called the Zephyr to pick up Dizzy and his musicians at New York's Pennsylvania Station. Before boarding, Dizzy went across the street to the Penta Hotel to receive a huge birthday cake. It took four chefs to carry the cake across the avenue to the train, with Dizzy and over one hundred musicians following the cake. The police stopped traffic to let the group cross. Dizzy got the bright idea to go to a newsstand and buy the *New York Post* to read on the train. When he turned left, all the musicians followed him. Dizzy's current manager, Charlie Fishman, watched in amazement and amusement as everyone followed Dizzy.

He could have retired, but instead he organized a big band in 1988—the United Nation Orchestra, he called it, because it had musicians from all over the world. (In 1989 it would make a recording, *Dizzy Gillespie and the United Nation Orchestra: Live at Royal Festival Hall in London*, which would win him a Grammy Award for 1991.) He was also always doing special concerts with all kinds of groups in important halls.

A famous jazz writer named Nat Hentoff wrote a story in the *Village Voice* about Dizzy that showed the power of his presence by then. Dizzy was supposed to lead a big band in a concert in his own honor at New York's Lincoln Center. A few days before the concert, Hentoff went to the rehearsal and found all the musicians in their places onstage. But Dizzy was not around. "No music was being played. The only sounds were a bitter argument" between two musicians, both of them big stars in jazz. Each one wanted more of his own compositions played in the concert. "Then [the argument] became very personal and poisonous," Hentoff wrote. The other musicians were embarrassed. "The tension in the room got fiercer and fiercer." Hentoff noticed Dizzy standing in the back of the hall. He was listening to the argument. "He strode to the front of the band, spread out a score, and said, 'Letter B, we'll start at Letter B.' " The moment they heard Dizzy's reasonable voice, the musicians stopped arguing. Other bandleaders might have scolded the musicians and added to the tension. But that was not Dizzy's style. "Softly, able to relax now, an alto saxophonist blew the rest of the bad feelings out the door, as he played, 'I'll Always Be in Love with You.' Even the two starring musicians who had been fighting laughed," Hentoff reported.

In 1989 Dizzy received the National Medal of the Arts

from the United States government. Another highlight of that year was a monthlong tour he made of Africa, during which he visited Morocco, Egypt, and Zaire. In Senegal Dizzy met the country's president. And in Nigeria Dizzy got one of the thrills of his life when he was installed as an African chieftain, with the title Bashere of Iperu. Always fascinated with his African heritage, he hoped to spend more time visiting Africa.

In 1990 he performed more than 250 concerts in twenty-seven countries. That was an amazing number for a man of any age. Some people said he actually played in 300 concerts. Among them were three days of concerts in East Berlin, Moscow, and Prague, Czechoslovakia, where the Czech president and U.S. ambassador Shirley Temple Black were his hosts. He flew in Air Force II with U.S. secretary of state James Baker to appear at the State Independence Banquet in Namibia, Africa. His manager noted proudly that Dizzy was the only artist invited to perform there.

In May 1990 he and Lorraine celebrated their fiftieth wedding anniversary. "I guess she must like my music," he commented to someone who asked him the secret of their successful, unconventional marriage.

On December 2, 1990, he went to Washington to receive the prestigious Kennedy Center Honors Award. Also getting their awards were actress Katharine Hepburn, opera star Risë Stevens, composer Jule Styne, and producer Billy Wilder. Dizzy talked most about meeting Katharine Hepburn. The National Academy of Recording Arts and Sciences gave him a Lifetime Achievement Award. It seemed as if everyone wanted to honor Dizzy.

During the summer of 1991, just before his seventy-fourth birthday, thousands of people showed up at the World Financial Center in Manhattan to hear him lead an outdoor concert. People waited for more than an hour, until his delayed flight arrived. As usual, he was on his way home from a tour. He made his way through city traffic to get to the bandstand. In the midst of that enormous crowd, he looked like a tiny speck. But he made a big, exciting noise. Two jazz musicians saw each other in the audience. Both played trumpet.

One said to the other, "We've come to hear our king."

15

dizzy's diamond anniversary

HE was on top of the world. In 1991 he toured Africa with singer Miriam Makeba, who first became famous for singing an African click song, making an incredible clicking noise with her mouth. The American Society of Composers, Authors and Publishers gave Dizzy the prestigious Duke Ellington Award. Dizzy and Max Roach collaborated on an album in Paris. They included a casual conversation about the old days when bebop was struggling for recognition. The album was nominated for a Grammy.

As soon as Dizzy turned seventy-four, everyone started rushing to congratulate him on his seventy-fifth birthday. It would be his diamond birthday celebration. Recordings were released and concerts were planned. He was still so entertaining that all he had to do was walk out onstage with his usual quick step at Carnegie Hall—or anyplace—and he made the place light up. Audiences cheered at the sight of him. He used some old jokes. They were still effective. One of the best ones was, "Ladies and gentlemen, I'd like to introduce the members of the band." Then he introduced the band members to one another. Audiences always howled with laughter.

Dizzy often made surprise appearances. He just walked out onstage as a guest during concerts that hadn't scheduled him. Often he hadn't planned to be a guest. But when he came home from someplace—Europe, Japan, he was not content to stay home and relax. He ran out again to play a little music for an audience. One summer he played in a concert as part of the annual JVC Jazz Festival concert, sponsored by the Japanese Victor Corporation, in New York City, along with his protégé, Jon Faddis, and another wonderful young trumpeter, Wynton Marsalis. Nobody could play better than those young men. But neither of them played better than Dizzy that night. Together, they brought cheers from the audience.

Dizzy was not having an easy time physically. He had another operation for cataracts in the early 1990s. He was still overeating, which was very bad for his diabetes, and he knew it. He showed up for a Carnegie Hall concert that honored Cab Calloway, who was then in his eighties. He and Cab hugged each other onstage. Audiences were touched. Dizzy looked young and spry.

But in December 1991, when he toured Japan, his manager, Charlie Fishman, noticed that Dizzy didn't have his usual energy. Charlie was used to seeing Dizzy get up early in the morning, eat, buy a paper, and take a walk. Sometimes Dizzy wandered around or went for a swim at a health club. But this trip, he was listless and slept late.

Early in 1992 Dizzy went to play at the Blue Note, a big, expensive jazz club in New York City where many of the most famous jazz musicians worked. He was scheduled to play for a month, spending a week with one group, then a week with another group, and then two more weeks with other groups. Dizzy stood in their midst and played a little bit, but he didn't always sound very forceful. During intermissions, when people went backstage to see him, he sometimes seemed a little cranky. He was eager to get his dinners served to him fast. He was looking for a way to boost his energy. "I'm hungry," he complained. He looked tired and overweight as he took the dinner plates heaped high with food and disappeared into a dressing room.

After he left the Blue Note, he was going to do one-night stands in Washington, D.C., Iowa, Pennsylvania, and six other places, then spend a week performing in Oakland, California, and then go on to Seattle, Washington. His only rest periods were the days he took for traveling between jobs. To Dizzy it was a normal schedule.

He was sitting in his dressing room just before he was supposed to go onstage in Oakland, and he couldn't get up. For the first time in his life, he said, "I can't." He didn't have the strength. He was feeling too sick.

He went to a hospital for two days of examinations. Doctors thought he might be troubled by his diabetes, and they advised him to go home for a thorough checkup. He felt strong enough to go back to work for two days in Oakland, then on to perform in Seattle. Lorraine waited at home, thinking about Dizzy's diabetes and how he ate whatever he pleased. Now she was terribly worried, she said. He came home to her, and then he went to the hospital for exploratory surgery. The doctors wanted to see exactly what was going on. They found out that Dizzy had pancreatic cancer.

At first he and Lorraine told friends that Dizzy was resting after the operation, and he would be okay. But months passed. It became clear that Dizzy wasn't getting well. He wasn't going out on the road to play anymore. Charlie Fishman wasn't sure if Dizzy had been told that he had cancer. Dizzy flew to the West Coast to make an appearance, but he didn't play. When he showed up next, at a concert in New York State, he looked very thin and weak. Then, for a while he seemed to be getting better, and he planned to go on a jazz cruise to the Caribbean. It was organized in his honor. But the doctors told him he shouldn't go. His seventy-fifth birthday came and went. Dizzy didn't play at a concert in his honor in New York.

At the end of the year, he was sick in bed at home. The phone rang, and Lorraine answered it. She was waiting for a call back from a doctor. But it wasn't the doctor calling. It was a writer who asked how everything was going. Lorraine and Dizzy got scores of phone calls every day. Lorraine rarely answered the phone anymore. Dizzy's nephew or an answering service usually took it. This time Lorraine was so anxious to get a call from the doctor that she picked up the phone herself. She said softly, "Well, I'm waiting for the doctor right now. Dizzy's not feeling very well, you know."

That day he went to Englewood hospital, and he stayed for a while. He joked with a nephew that he was "too famous to die." One day while there, Dizzy was sitting up in a chair, talking to Jon Faddis, who was visiting him. Mike Longo (a pianist who had worked with Dizzy for years), saxophonist James Moody, and a friend from Switzerland were there, too. Dizzy drifted off to sleep. He never woke up.

Newspapers, magazines, and television announced Dizzy's death on January 6, 1993. Many people had known and loved Dizzy. They told all kinds of stories about him. Some were funny, some were impressive.

One writer recalled that she had called Dizzy for an interview. He answered his home telephone himself. The writer asked him if he would answer some questions. He said, "Why didn't you call me on my office phone?" The writer said she only had the one phone number, which had been given to her by a photographer. "I'm so sorry to bother you," she said. "If you give me your office number, I'll call you back there." Dizzy boomed, "I don't have an office!" And then he chuckled.

Charlie Fishman recalled how a reporter asked Dizzy what advice he could give young people, and Dizzy replied, "Don't be a backbiter." Don't say bad things about people behind their backs. Tell them what you have to say to their faces, or don't say anything at all. Fishman couldn't forget these words of wisdom. It seemed impossible to believe that Dizzy was dead.

A church service took place at St. Peter's Lutheran Church in Manhattan the next week. A few days later six thousand people crowded into one of the largest cathedrals in the United States, the Episcopal Cathedral of St. John the Divine in Morningside Heights in New York. Wynton Marsalis led a New Orleans–style funeral parade around the cathedral. Singer Roberta Flack, who had known Dizzy for years, sang "Amazing Grace" in a rich contralto voice for one of the most beautiful performances of her career. Musicians who had known Dizzy all their adult lives met one another in the packed aisles of the cathedral. They comforted one another by saying, "Bird was calling him."

suggested listening

MOST of Dizzy Gillespie's recordings are available from one source or another. They're on cassettes, long-playing records (LPs), and compact discs (CDs). Any recording released in recent years is on cassettes and CDs only. Relatively few of his old, historic recordings released on LPs have been reissued on CDs. If you live near a secondhand record store that sells old LPs, you'll be able to find some of Dizzy's recordings from the 1940s. You'll especially want to look for LPs and cassettes of songs that Dizzy and Charlie Parker played together.

Available on the Musicraft Records label is *Dizzy Gillespie and His Sextets*, recordings from 1945 and 1946. On it are seven songs featuring Dizzy and Bird: "Groovin' High," "Dizzy Atmosphere," "All the Things You Are," "Shaw Nuff," "Lover Man," "Salt Peanuts," and "Hot House," recorded in February and May 1945.

Libraries with recordings, such as the New York Public Library for the Performing Arts at Lincoln Center in New York City, have copies available for listening. Also, schools and universities with jazz departments have historic Dizzy Gillespie recordings. You may visit these libraries, usually by appointment. If you don't live nearby, you can usually write for taped copies. For a small charge the schools will send you cassettes of recordings not available through record stores.

Music stores selling newly issued recordings on CDs carry three important albums:

1. ***Jazz at Massey Hall,*** the concert played by Dizzy with Bird, Max Roach, Bud Powell, and Charles Mingus, recorded in 1953 for the Debut label, now available on the Original Jazz Classics label.
2. ***Groovin' High,*** recorded in 1956, with Dizzy Gillespie and the big band that represented the United States and toured Asia and the Near East first, then South America in 1956. It's on the Bandstand label.
3. ***Max Plus Dizzy,*** A&M Records, recorded in Paris in 1989, with Dizzy and Max Roach.

There are countless recordings of Dizzy with many groups at jazz festivals, and in concerts. Among Dizzy's last recordings are *To Bird with Love,* recorded on January

23–25, 1992, on the Telarc label, and *To Diz with Love*, recorded live at the Blue Note jazz club, January 29–31, 1992, featuring a collection of great trumpeters.

bibliography

Dance, Stanley. *The World of Earl Hines*. New York: Charles Scribner's Sons, 1977.

Feather, Leonard. *Inside Jazz*. New York: Da Capo Press, 1977. (Originally published as *Inside Bebop* by J. J. Robbins and Sons, 1949.)

Giddins, Gary. *Celebrating Bird: The Triumph of Charlie Parker*. New York: Beech Tree Books–Quill, 1987.

Gillespie, Dizzy, with Al Fraser. *To BE or Not . . . to BOP*. New York: Doubleday, 1979.

Gitler, Ira. *Swing to Bop: An Oral History of the Transition in Jazz in the 1940s*. New York: Oxford University Press, 1985.

Lees, Gene. *Waiting for Dizzy*. New York: Oxford University Press, 1991.

Stokes, W. Royal. *The Jazz Scene*. New York: Oxford University Press, 1991.

A variety of periodicals has been consulted for background. The magazines are *Playboy*, *Metronome*, *Down Beat*, *Esquire*, *Melody Maker*, *Carolina Lifestyle*, the *New Yorker*, *Vis-a-Vis*, *TWA Ambassador*, and *Diversion*. Newspapers include the *New York Times*, the *Daily News*, the *New York Post*, and the *Village Voice*, all in New York City; and the *International Herald Tribune*, published in Paris.

Special thanks to the Institute of Jazz Studies, Rutgers University, for its generous assistance with its files on Dizzy Gillespie. The town of Cheraw, South Carolina, has provided photographic reference materials from files on the town's history and also newspaper stories that appeared in Cheraw and in Charlotte, North Carolina.

Of great help have been radio interviews with Dizzy Gillespie and other musicians for Dizzy's fiftieth anniversary as a recording artist celebrated on WKCR in 1987, with Phil Schaap as host, and "Dizzy's Diamond," a series on WNYC in 1992. Excerpts from those broadcasts have been incorporated in the book.

Recommended as a study aid is the video "Dizzy Gillespie: A Night in Tunisia," issued by V.I.E.W. Video, Inc. (34 East Twenty-third Street, New York, NY 10010, phone [212] 674-5550), on which Dizzy plays piano and explains how he composed the song. There's also a vivid portrayal of Dizzy playing trumpet, with his cheeks blown up like big balloons. V.I.E.W. Video has also released other videos of Dizzy, for example, "Dizzy Gillespie: A Night in Chicago." Another video is "Dizzy Gillespie: The Dizzy Gillespie Ages," issued by Green Line Video in 1990.

index